WEEKLY THEMES

for ASSEMBLIES

Phil Grice

Heinemann

This book is dedicated to my Mum and Dad and daughter, Hannah.

Heinemann Educational Publishers
Halley Court, Jordan Hill, Oxford OX2 8EJ
a division of Reed Educational & Professional Publishing Ltd

MADRID   ATHENS   PARIS
FLORENCE   PRAGUE   WARSAW
PORTSMOUTH NH   CHICAGO   SAO PAULO
SINGAPORE   TOKYO   MELBOURNE   AUCKLAND
IBADAN   GABORONE   JOHANNESBURG

© Phil Grice 1996

First published 1996

99 98 97 96
10 9 8 7 6 5 4 3 2 1

British Library Cataloguing in Publication Data
A catalogue record for this book is available from the British Library

ISBN 0 435 30246 9

Designed by Aricot Vert Design
Typeset by Books Unlimited (Nottm)
Printed and bound in Great Britain by Clays Ltd, St Ives plc

Acknowledgements

I would like to thank Fr. Philip Inch, Br. Ligouri Gillespie and the staff and pupils at St. Cuthbert's R C Community High School for their help and contributions. Particular thanks go to my wife, Anne, for her advice and patience.

The publishers would like to thank the following for the use of copyright material reproduced in this book:
Amnesty International and Terry Waite for the extract on pp. 55–6; The Bible Society/HarperCollins Publishers Ltd, for scriptures quoted from *The Good News Bible*, UK © American Bible Society 1966, 1971, 1976, 1992; used with permission on pp. 20–21, 28–9, 31–2, 34–5, 36–7, 41, 43–4, 45–6, 51–2, 54–5, 61, 67–8, 74, 82–3, 85–6, 88–9, 94–5, 102–3, 108–9; Michael Buerk for the account of the Ethiopian famine on pp. 37–8; Ann Byre for the extract from *Here I Am*, published by HarperCollins, © Ann Byre 1992 on p. 21; CAFOD for extracts from *Celebrating One World* on pp. 19, 22–3, 32; Tony Castle for the extract from *Assemble Together*, reproduced by permission of Geoffrey Chapman, an imprint of Cassell, London, on p. 98; Brian Clough for the extract from *Clough the Autobiography* published by Partridge Press, an imprint of Transworld Publishers. © Brian Clough 1994. All rights reserved, on p. 126; Anthony De Mello for the extract 'Khrushchev in Congress Hall' from *The Song of the Bird*, published by Image Books, reproduced by permission of Reed Books, on pp. 77, and for the extract from *The Prayer of the Frog*, published by HarperCollins, on pp. 86–7; Brian Flynn for the letter from the *Liverpool Echo* on p. 128; The Grail Community for the 'Grail Prayer' on p. 84; T.C. Hamlet for the adapted extract 'Frogs in Cream' taken from the book *Frogs in Cream*, published and reproduced by permission of Scripture Union, on p. 44; Quotes from 1988 Educational Reform Act & Circular 'Religious Education and Collective Worship 1/94', Crown copyright, reproduced by permission of the Controller of Her Majesty's Stationery Office, on pp. 5–6; Hodder Headline plc/International Bible Society for extracts from the *New International Version* of the Bible on pp. 17, 48–9, 59–60, 64–5, 70–1, 72, 76–7, 80, 91, 97–8, 105–6; The Estate of Martin Luther King for extracts from *Stride Toward Freedom*, published by HarperRow Inc on pp. 23–4, 41–2, 103; Penguin Books for the extract from *The Brothers Karamazov* by Dostoyevsky on p. 79; Piper/Pan Macmillan for the poem by Lotte Moos from *Can You Hear Poems* on p. 58; Jonathan Porritt for the extract from *Save the Planet* published by Dorling Kindersley Ltd, © Jonathan Porritt 1991; Reed International Books, for extracts from *The Prophet* by Kahlil Gibran on pp. 17–18, 109–10; Lyrics from the song 'The Living Years' by Mike and The Mechanics, © 1988 Michael Rutherford Ltd/ R & BA Music Ltd/Hit & Run Music (Publishing) Ltd. International Copyright Secured. All rights reserved. Used by permission, on p. 127; Sidgewick & Jackson for the extract from *Is That It?* by Bob Gedolf on p. 83; Tabor Publishing for the extract from a story by Mark Link from *Decision* on p. 95; Twenty-Third Publications for the extract by Bausch from *Storytelling, Imagination and Faith* on pp. 100–1; Vallentine, Mitchell & Co. Ltd for the extract from *The Diary of Anne Frank*, 1954, on p. 71; W. Wilcock for extracts from *One More Step* published and reproduced by permission of Stanley Thornes (Publishers) Ltd on p. 88; Chris Wright for extracts from *Key Christian Beliefs* © Lion Publishing plc, on pp. 22, 68–9.

The publishers have made every effort to trace copyright holders. However, if any material has been incorrectly acknowledged, we would be pleased to correct this at the earliest opportunity.

Contents

SPECIFIC THEMES

SPECIAL THEMES

Introduction

Since the publication of the 1988 Education Reform Act the issue of Collective Worship has been at the forefront of debate in schools and the media. There has been uncertainty about how the law can best be implemented to ensure that acts of worship are a relevant, significant and life-giving experience to pupils. This book aims to provide a pathway through this uncertainty from an understanding of the legal requirements to creating a collective worship policy to implementing an effective worship programme. The bulk of the book provides material linked to a pattern of weekly themes. The material can be used by a tutor to provide form-based worship or as a resource to provoke ideas for year or whole-school assemblies.

What does the Law say?

The 1988 Education Reform Act laid down the requirements for Collective Worship in maintained schools. 'Religious Education and Collective Worship' (Circular 1/94) gives further guidance.

The requirements for maintained schools can be summarised as follows.

- All pupils should take part in an act of Collective Worship on each school day.
- The act of Collective Worship can take place at any time during the school day.
- There is no requirement for the whole school to meet together for Collective Worship. The organisation is flexible and can take place in whatever grouping the school decides (with the exception of faith groups). In other words Collective Worship can take place in year groups, form groups, or even English sets but not, for example, as an Anglican group.

- The statutory act of Collective Worship must take place on school premises. Additional acts of Collective Worship may be arranged outside of school.
- In any one term most acts of Collective Worship should be wholly or mainly of a broadly Christian character. They should reflect the broad traditions of Christian belief but must not be distinctive of any one Christian denomination.
- In all acts of Collective Worship account should be taken of the ages, aptitudes and family background of the pupils.
- If a school considers worship that is wholly or mainly of a broadly Christian character is inappropriate then an application for a determination can be made to the local SACRE (Standing Advisory Council on Religious Education). This would enable an alternative worship structure to take place.
- Parents have the right to withdraw their children from acts of Collective Worship (and RE).
- Teachers also have the right to withdraw from attending Collective Worship.

Understanding the Law

WHY THE TERM 'COLLECTIVE WORSHIP'?

'Assembly' is the word that pupils and teachers alike have used to describe worship within schools. Yet the Education Acts of 1944 and 1988 use the term Collective Worship in preference to assembly. The distinction is more than one of semantics. Assembly is a coming together of a specific group within the school. It may involve sharing information, presentation of awards, warnings to and criticism of individuals or whole groups. Collective Worship, however, is the explicit act of worship that may be carried out within an assembly. It is an occasion that focuses on specifically spiritual matters. Often there is a tension caused by having the act of Collective Worship within the context of an assembly as the two may not always be compatible.

WHY 'COLLECTIVE'?

In the initial debate in the 1944 Act the term Corporate Worship was replaced by Collective Worship. Corporate Worship implies that there is a body of believers who share a commitment to a particular faith – it demands a common set of beliefs and attitudes. This is clearly inappropriate within a county school and hence the continued use of the term Collective not Corporate Worship.

WHAT IS WORSHIP?

Various meanings and interpretations have been given to the word 'worship'. In its strictly religious sense worship would refer to the adoration by believers. Within a faith community it could refer to the rituals, beliefs, prayer or celebrations of the particular denomination or faith.

The actual word 'worship' derives from the Anglo-Saxon, 'weorthscipe', meaning honour or 'worth-ship'. It is probably this definition that is an appropriate starting point for describing acts of worship within a county school. This definition allows worship to be considered as examining all that is of value and honour; and exploring the spiritual dimension of life. For the believer this exploration would be within the understanding that the focus for worship is God.

The nature of worship will vary greatly depending on the context of the school but, whatever its nature, for worship to have integrity it must enable pupils to have a free response. In short, 'A school is not a worshipping community...but rather a worship enabling community'. (*Schools for Tomorrow*, ed. B. O'Keefe, Falmer Press)

'COLLECTIVE WORSHIP SHOULD BE WHOLLY OR MAINLY OF A BROADLY CHRISTIAN CHARACTER'

Circular 1/94 interprets this phrase by suggesting that:

- Collective Worship should reflect the broad traditions of Christian belief but not be distinctive of a particular denomination.
- Schools may have acts of worship that are in the tradition of other religions or may have elements drawn from a number of faiths. However over the course of a term the majority of acts of worship should be wholly or mainly of a broadly Christian character.
- Acts of worship may include non-Christian material or include material that is embraced by people of many faiths. It must,

however, contain some elements that relate specifically to the traditions of the Christian belief and which accord a special status to Jesus Christ.

- Collective Worship should be open to all and should not exclude pupils from non-Christian families.
- It is suggested that the headteacher ensures that a record is kept of the daily acts of worship.

THE CHURCH SCHOOL

In a church, independent or voluntary aided school the legal situation differs from maintained schools. The responsibility for Collective Worship lies with the governors in consultation with the headteacher and denominational worship is permitted. Although the nature, character and style of worship may be different many of the aims, principles and practices are identical.

MULTI-FAITH COLLECTIVE WORSHIP

If a school considers that collective worship that is wholly or mainly Christian is inappropriate then the Head and governors may apply to their local SACRE for a determination. For those schools who do not seek a determination, especially in multi-racial, multi-faith areas, there is a need to ensure that acts of worship respect the integrity of *all* involved.

Creating a policy statement

It is essential that each school has a clear policy statement that sets out the aims and principles of worship as well as giving details of the strategies that are employed to ensure that Collective Worship is a vibrant and worthwhile activity. It is important that all are involved and are aware of the procedures for Collective Worship in the school.

Whether as a school you are writing a new policy or reviewing the existing one the guidelines below are offered as a focus for discussions.

The suggested framework for a policy is:

Aims: What does the school hope to achieve through Collective Worship?

Principles: What are the beliefs that the school holds about Collective Worship?

Strategies: How will Collective Worship be co-ordinated, organised, resourced, planned and evaluated?

Conclusion: A summary statement of the nature, character and value of Collective Worship.

In drawing up the policy copies of *Spiritual and Moral Development – A discussion paper* (NCC, 1993), the 1988 ERA and Circular 1/94 will prove valuable.

AIMS

The aims of Collective Worship will be specific to each school. To establish those suitable for your school you could begin by considering each of the aims listed below. Which are essential, which are not relevant and which do you consider need further discussion and thought?

a) to explore social, moral and spiritual values

b) to consider and celebrate the values of the Christian Gospels

c) to encourage an understanding of religious beliefs and practices

d) to consider and celebrate the richness of Christianity and of other faith traditions

e) to develop a sense of community

f) to affirm and develop the individual

g) to offer opportunities for reflection, meditation and prayer

h) to develop a sense of enquiry and to encourage a search for human meaning

i) to foster a sense of joy, awe and wonder in creation

j) to experience the sacred and to develop an awareness of the presence of God in others and in oneself

k) to appreciate symbolism and ritual as aspects of worship

l) to encourage an awareness of and a compassion for the needs of the world community

PRINCIPLES

What are the principles on which Collective Worship is to be founded? Again each of the following suggestions could be a starting point.

Collective Worship should be:

- an educational activity linked to the whole curriculum
- memorable and enjoyable
- designed to actively engage pupils, and elicit responses
- resourced and planned
- flexible and able to respond to special occasions
- related to the age, ability and background of pupils
- a sense of occasion
- inclusive and not confessional

STRATEGIES

It is the intention of this book to help in the planning of Collective Worship by providing a framework for delivery and support materials for both tutorial worship and assemblies. Answers to the following questions should serve to form the basis of the strategies for Collective Worship in your school.

Co-ordination
1. Who will have overall responsibility?
2. Will a Collective Worship planning group be established?

Organisation
1. What venues and groupings of pupils will be used (form, year, whole school or a mixture)?
2. Will Collective Worship be carried out within assembly time? If so, will any guidance be given to staff as to how to make a distinction between the 'business' and 'worship' elements of assembly?

Resources
1. Are existing resources catalogued?
2. How do you ensure that resources are sufficiently used – is there, for example, a brief summary of each assembly book?
3. Has use been made of information from aid agencies, newspapers, magazines?
4. Are pupils involved in developing resources (especially music)?
5. Are departments able to contribute to the stock of resources?
6. Is there any additional funding available to buy new resources?

Planning
1. How will you ensure that Collective Worship is:

- educational
- a planned and balanced experience for pupils
- wholly or mainly of a broadly Christian character?

Would a pattern of weekly themes help to ensure these features?

2. If weekly themes are used will there be flexibility to respond to unforeseen events – e.g. a time of disaster or of celebration?
3. How can form tutors be supported in delivering Collective Worship in the classroom?
4. Will Collective Worship journals (see next section) be used to enable pupils to take an active role in tutor based Collective Worship?
5. Will pupils be involved in the planning, preparation and delivery of acts of Worship?
6. What support will be given to teachers delivering Collective Worship to year, house or whole-school groups?
7. How will you ensure that there is a balance and variety in the styles of Collective Worship?
8. Will the skills of delivering meaningful Collective Worship be shared in INSET time?
9. Will visitors help to deliver Collective Worship? If so, what guidance will be given to ensure that the assembly is appropriate and relevant? Can you collaborate with neighbouring schools to establish a list of people who would be willing and able to be a part of a school Collective Worship programme?

Recording and Evaluation
1. What methods will you use to record and evaluate Collective Worship? (A suggested Recording and Evaluation sheet is provided on page 12.)
2. How will the findings of your evaluation be used to further develop the quality of worship in school?

CONCLUSION
The conclusion should, very briefly, serve to summarise the aims, principles and strategies of Collective Worship. An indication should be given of the particular nature and character of worship within the school and of the value and importance placed upon it.

Collective Worship Record Sheet

Teacher	Week no. & date

Theme

Aim(s)

Style (Tick one or more)

Scripture	☐	Drama	☐	Visual aids	☐
Dance	☐	Creative silence	☐	Other (Please give	
Meditation	☐	Artefacts	☐	details below)	☐
Video	☐	Music	☐		
Prayer	☐	Story & Readings	☐		

Brief Description

    Tick if pupils were involved in:

    Planning the assembly   ☐

    Taking an active part in the assembly

    (e.g. reading, drama etc.)   ☐

Evaluation (If appropriate, include staff or pupil comments)

Using this book

This book provides 39 themes for Collective Worship in secondary schools, one for each week of the school year. The majority of the themes are of a broadly Christian character in keeping with the 1988 Education Reform Act. The book contains 'General Themes', which can be used at any time of the year, 'Specific Themes', which refer to particular festivals, seasons or occasions and 'Special Themes', which involve a greater level of preparation and involvement. This format enables individual schools to establish their own pattern of themes for the year.

The themes could be used to provide a focus for the act of worship within an assembly as well as providing support for tutor based collective worship. In addition the five Special Themes allow pupils to explore Collective Worship in a more active way.

GENERAL AND SPECIFIC THEMES

There are 34 general and specific themes. Each of these explore major life themes, festivals and beliefs and try to cover many of the main aims and principles of Collective Worship. Each theme has the same general format:

- Introduction to the theme.
- Relevant reading from scriptures.
- Story – a rich selection of stories, taken from a wide range of sources.
- Activity – for pupils to reflect on the theme.
- Prayer.

This format ensures that each theme provides enough resources for 4–5 tutor group acts of worship of about two minutes in length. The themes can be used directly with classes or alternatively used as a framework upon which the teacher can develop classroom worship appropriate to the age, ability and experiences of the pupils.

SPECIAL THEMES

The activities in the general and specific themes ensure that pupils are not just passive receivers of Collective Worship. In addition, the programme provided here includes 'Special Themes' that further encourage involvement through the use of symbolism, imagery, gesture, music or silence and meditation to explore the theme. Each of the special themes have clear directions for teachers which provide guidance and details of resources required.

These special themes need a greater degree of thought and planning and need some simple resources but they will help ensure that Collective Worship is truly a life-giving experience for pupils and not just an exercise to fulfil a statutory requirement. It is suggested that a Collective Worship co-ordinator organises and resources each of these special themes. As the themes can be adapted for use throughout a secondary school, they could be arranged on a rota basis for the year groups so that resources and organisation can be kept to a minimum.

Tutor-group acts of worship
A SUGGESTED FORMAT FOR USING THE THEMES

Opening
Introduce the worship theme for the week.

Input
The resources from the weekly theme could be used. An introduction would help, e.g. 'This reading is taken from…,
A pattern for the week could be:

> **Day 1:** Based on the introduction
> **Day 2:** The Story
> **Day 3**: The Reading from Scripture
> **Day 4:** The Activity

A piece of quiet, reflective music could be played in the background and may be particularly useful during an activity.

Reflection
You may wish to share your own thoughts relating to the week's theme: the Radio 4 programme *Thought for the Day* provides a useful model. Alternatively, there could be a small group or class discussion based on the passage or activity. You may also wish to

have a time of creative silence for personal prayer and reflection.

Prayer
You could conclude the act of worship with a well-known prayer, the prayer from the theme or with prayers written by pupils.

INVOLVING PUPILS
Ideally pupils should be fully involved in the planning, preparation and delivery of acts of Collective Worship. In the first instance this may involve pupils reading passages but as they become familiar with the pattern of worship this could be developed so that pupils customise the theme. Pupils may wish to suggest and provide relevant and recent pieces of music or could explore the theme through mime, drama or art.

Some of the following suggestions may also prove useful.

- Write out and display the pattern of themes for the term.
- Create and display a rota of pupils willing to lead the acts of worship.
- Have this book and other assembly resources displayed and available for pupil use.
- Have a 'Worship Wall' and display newspaper articles and pictures, pupils' prayers and the plan of themes for the term.
- Use centring objects during worship such as a candle, cross or other religious artefact.
- Involve pupils in reviewing and evaluating acts of worship.

Above all be adventurous, a daily act of worship should not just be a statutory requirement but an integral element of the religious, spiritual and moral life of the school. Pupils are not looking for text-book worship nor sentimentality but for 'genuine conviction and evidence of someone else embarked on a spiritual journey and able to some extent to articulate it.' (Cope, Lundy and McKeore)

COLLECTIVE WORSHIP JOURNAL
Collective Worship journals can be a worthwhile addition to a worship programme in schools. Workbooks or a section in a PSE file/folder could be used to record pupils' thoughts and reflections on the worship theme for that week. On many occasions the activity section could provide a focus for this reflection or alterna-

tively pupils could be encouraged to write down what they have learnt or discovered in relation to that particular theme.

Five minutes of a PSE or pastoral period could be set aside for the journal writing with some feedback or discussion where appropriate.

Having a book that provides a focus for Collective Worship enables both pupil and form tutor to see a pattern of growth in spiritual development as well as opening up another avenue of communication between teacher and pupil.

1 • Giving

Introduction

A plumber once said that people could be described as either drains or radiators. Drains were people who constantly took, they would speak only of themselves and their problems. Radiators were the natural givers in life – people who could not help but radiate joy and happiness.

In the extract from Kahlil Gibran's *The Prophet* we hear that 'Through the hands of such as these God speaks, and from behind their eyes He smiles upon the earth.'

Scripture

The reading is from *Mark 12*. Jesus speaks about true giving, it is not giving of your excess or making a show of the giving but about sacrificing what you have for others. In this way the two small coins of the window are 'worth more' than the whole amount thrown in by the rich people.

> Jesus sat down opposite the place where the offerings were put and watched the crowd putting their money into the temple treasury. Many rich people threw in large amounts.
>
> But a poor widow came and put in two very small copper coins, worth only a fraction of a penny.
>
> Calling his disciples to him, Jesus said, 'I tell you the truth, this poor widow has put more into the treasury than all the others.
>
> They all gave out of their wealth; but she, out of her poverty, put in everything – all she had to live on.'

Story

The following extract is from *The Prophet* by Kahlil Gibran.

> Then says a rich man, Speak to us of Giving. And he answered:
> You give little when you give of your possessions.
> It is when you give of yourself that you truly give...
> There are those who give little of the much which they have – and they give it for recognition and their hidden desire makes their gifts unwholesome.
> And there are those who have little and give it all. These are the believers in life and the bounty of life, and their coffer is never empty.
> There are those who give with joy, and that joy is their reward.
> And there are those who give with pain, and that pain is their baptism...
> And there are those who give and know not pain in giving, nor do they seek joy, nor give with mindfulness of virtue;
> They give as in yonder valley the myrtle breathes its fragrance into space.
> Through the hands of such as these God speaks, and from behind their eyes He smiles upon the earth.

Activity

Time should be given for pupils to reflect on the following.

Describe an occasion where you have given 'something of yourself'.

Read again the extract from *The Prophet*. Which type of giver are you and why?

Prayer

The following Quaker prayer explores what it means to give.

Lord, when I am hungry
Give me someone to feed;
When I am thirsty
Give water for their thirst.
When I am sad
Someone to lift from sorrow.
When burden weighs upon me
Lay upon my shoulders
The burden of my fellows,

Lord, when I stand
Greatly in need of tenderness,
Give me someone who yearns
For love. May your will
Be my bread; your grace
My strength; your love
My resting place.

2 • Community

Introduction

When we have toothache or a headache it is hard to ignore it. We cannot pretend that part of our body is not there; for it only takes one part of our body to be hurting for us to feel unwell.

St. Paul compares communities to bodies, every part being as important as another. We are all members of communities, in our families and in our schools. We all belong and each has a role to play. Just as a body needs **every** part, within a community **each person** is important and unique and should be valued.

Scripture

The reading is from *1 Corinthians 12*. St. Paul is telling the people of Corinth not to argue over who is the greatest, or who is the most talented, but to realise that, with God, each person is valued equally, and each person has a unique role to play in the community.

Just as Christ is like a single body, which has many parts; it is still one body, even though it is made up of different parts. In the same way, all of us, whether Jews or Gentiles, whether slave or free, we have been baptised into the same body, by the same Spirit, and we have all been given the one Spirit to drink.

For the body itself is not made up of only one part, but of many parts...

God put every different part in the body just as He wanted it to be. There would not be a body if it were all only one part! As it is there are many parts but the one body.

Story

A Japanese husband stood with his wife and their son and daughter on the platform at a meeting. In staccato English he said, 'I am father. I am like coconut. Hard outside – soft inside. This is mother. She is like peach. Soft and lovely outside – hard inside.

This is son. He is like banana. Soft outside, soft inside, not straight and very slippery. This is daughter, She is like chestnut. Prickly outside and explodes when heated.

But now we are all changed. We make good fruit salad.'

Activity

Give pupils the following questions. Ask them to share their answers in small groups.

If you had to describe yourself as a type of fruit, what would it be and why?

Think about the communities that you belong to. What gifts and benefits do you bring to each community?

Prayer

We pray for the wisdom to understand that we are one body and to realise that when we hurt a part of that body we hurt ourselves, but when we each work for the good of each other the body is whole and strong. We pray that our school community grows in strength and unity.

3 • Despair

Introduction

There is a story of a man who slipped when walking along the edge of a cliff. As he fell he clung with his finger tips to the very edge of the cliff face.

'Help me,' he shouted. 'Is anyone there?'

'It's OK,' a voice said from far below. 'Just let go and I'll catch you'.

A few seconds passed and then the man shouted again, 'Is anyone else there?'

Often in the lives of great religious people it is in the moment of greatest despair that they have found their true strength – it is then that they learn to let go and to trust fully in God.

Scripture

The reading is from a Namibian adaptation of *Psalm 7*.

In this hour of despair and hopelessness
I come to you for comfort;
rescue me from my despair and give me faith, hope and
love,
else I will not be able to participate in your saving work
in the world;
I will from weariness collapse and die.

O Lord, my God, if I in my despair wronged anyone,
if I let a friend down or hurt in my impatience those who
love me –
If I have done any of these things,

then do not leave me in my guilt to endless grief.
Forgive, O Lord, forgive me and restore me to your love...

I thank you, Lord, for I know that you are at work;
you hold the whole world in your hands and you can change it.
I will sing your praises at all times.

Story

This extract from the book *Stride Toward Freedom* by Martin Luther King tells of the despair that Dr. King felt but also of his total faith and trust in God.

One night toward the end of January I settled into bed after a strenuous day. Coretta had fallen asleep and just as I was about to doze off the telephone rang. An angry voice said 'Listen, nigger, we've taken all we want from you; before next week you'll be sorry you ever came to Montgomery.'

I hung up, I could not sleep. It seemed that all my fears had come down on me at once. I had reached the saturation point. I got out of bed and began to walk the floor. Finally, I went to the kitchen and heated a pot of coffee. I was ready to give up. With my cup of coffee sitting untouched before me I tried to think of a way to move out of the picture without appearing a coward. In this state of exhaustion, when my courage had all but gone, I decided to take my problem to God. With my head in my hands, I bowed over the kitchen table and prayed aloud. The words I spoke to God that midnight are still vivid in my memory.

'I am here taking a stand for what I believe is right. But now I am afraid. The people are looking to me for leadership, and if I stand before them without strength and courage, they too will falter. I am at the end of my powers. I have nothing left. I've come to the point where I can't face it alone.'

> At that moment I experienced the presence of the Divine as I had never experienced him before.

Activity

Each of the games below could be used as a starting point for a discussion on trust, despair and faith.

Trust Walk

One pupil should be blindfolded and guided through a series of obstacles by a classmate who he or she can trust.

Trust Fall

One pupil should stand straight with arms outstretched with his or her back to another pupil. The first pupil should then fall slowly into the arms of the other pupil.

Pupils could then discuss the following questions.

How does it feel to 'let go' and put your trust in someone else?
Have you ever trusted anyone with something very important?
Have you ever felt in total despair?
Have you ever felt the help of God in the same way as Martin Luther King?

Prayer

> We pray that in our times of greatest despair we learn to trust fully in you.

4 • Wonder

Introduction

It's very easy to ignore the beauty and wonder of the world. Louis Armstrong's song, *What a Wonderful World,* asks us to look at the simple beauty of nature, the trees that are green, red roses, the brightness of day and the darkness of night, the sound of a baby crying or the sight of friends shaking hands. In the hustle and bustle of daily lives it is easy to forget to look with awe at the miracles of life all around us.

Scripture

These words from *Psalm 8* express the wonder that the writer feels for the world and its creator.

When I look at the sky, which you have made,
at the moon and the stars, which you set in their places –
what is man, that you think of him;
mere man, that you care for him?

Yet you made him inferior only to yourself;
you crowned him with glory and honour.

You appointed him ruler over everything you made;
you placed him over all creation:
sheep and cattle, and the wild animals too;
the birds and the fish
and the creatures in the seas.

O LORD, our Lord,
your greatness is seen in all the world!

Story

If the Earth were only a few feet in diameter, floating a few feet above a field somewhere, people would come from everywhere to marvel at it. People would walk around it marvelling at its big pools of water, its little pools and the water flowing between. People would marvel at the bumps on it and the holes in it. They would marvel at the very thin layer of gas surrounding it and the water suspended in the gas.

The people would marvel at all the creatures walking around the surface of the ball and at the creatures in the water. The people would declare it as sacred because it was the only one, and they would protect it so that it would not be hurt. The ball would be the greatest wonder known, and people would come to pray to it, to be healed, to gain knowledge, to know beauty and to wonder how it could be.

People would love it and defend it with their lives because they would somehow know that their lives could be nothing without it.

If the Earth were only a few feet in diameter.

Activity

Global Prayer

Pupils should write a prayer about the wonder of the world. The prayer could be written within a circle.

Prayer

We pray that we learn to have a love of our world, and that we look upon each aspect of creation with awe and with wonder.

5 • Gifts and talents

Introduction

When the footballer Diego Maradona was sent home from the 1994 World Cup for drug use, the newspapers and television all spoke about the huge waste of talent. However it is not just stars who can waste talent. Experts estimate that the average person achieves only 10% of their potential. In other words most of us squander or ignore 90% of our abilities. Now and again we come across people who fulfil their potential, who achieve something extraordinary. These people can be inspirations to us all.

Scripture

The reading is based on *Matthew 25:14–30*. Jesus told the parable so that people would use the talents that they have been given.

Jesus said, 'A man had three servants. He went away and left five silver coins with one of them, two silver coins with another and one silver coin with the third. While the master was away the servants worked.

When the master returned he asked: "What have you done with my coins?" The one who had received five said: "You gave me five, I have traded with them and now I have ten!"

The master was pleased: "I will give you more important work to do!" The one who had received two said: "You gave me two, by trading I have gained another two!"

Again the master said: "You have worked well with a little, I will give you more!"

The one who had received one coin said "You gave me one coin, I buried it. I was afraid I might lose it. Here I have dug it up for you."

The master said, "Lazy and thoughtless servant. You could have put it in the bank, at least it would have gained interest."'

Story

At the age of 7, Glenn Cunningham's legs were so severely burned that doctors considered amputation. At the last minute they decided against it. One of the doctors patted Glenn's shoulder: 'When the weather turns warm we'll get you into a chair on the porch.'

'I don't want to sit. I want to walk and run and I will.' There was no doubt in Glenn's voice. The doctor walked away.

Two years later, Glenn was running. The boy was not running fast, but he was running.

Eventually, Glenn went to college where he ran for the college team. No longer was he running to prove doctors wrong; now he was running because he was good at it. Soon college records began to fall under his driving legs. Then came the Berlin Olympics. Glenn not only qualified and ran in them, but also broke the Olympic record for the 1500 metre race.

The following year, Glenn broke the world's indoor-mile record. The boy who wasn't supposed to walk again became the world's fastest human in the indoor mile.

Activity

This exercise works best in groups of 5 or 6. Pupils should be given the following instructions.

1. Write your name on the bottom of a sheet of paper.
2. Pass the paper to the person on your left. Each person in the

group should then have a sheet with someone else's name on it.

3. At the very top of the sheet of paper write down some of the gifts and talents of the person whose name is on the sheet. It is important that you write only positive comments.

4. Fold the top strip of the paper over so your comments cannot be seen.

5. Pass the sheet to the person on the left.

Repeat steps 2 to 5 until you receive your own sheet.

Prayer

We pray in thanks for the gifts and talents that we have been given. May we learn to use these talents to the full.

6 • Violence

Introduction

Violence so often leads to more violence. People wish to gain revenge, to get their own back, to prove their strength or superiority. Now and again there have been people who have shown that real strength lies in non-violence.

This doesn't involve submission or accepting injustice but entails a passive resistance and a determination to fight wrong-doing through peaceful means.

Mahatma Gandhi is probably one of the most potent symbols of non-violence. His often quoted words sum up the futility of the cycle of violence: 'An eye for an eye and soon the whole world will be blind!'

Scripture

The reading is from *Matthew 26:47–54*. Even at the moment of his betrayal and arrest Jesus condemns retribution and violence.

Jesus was still speaking when Judas, one of the twelve disciples arrived. With him was a large crowd armed with swords and clubs and sent by the chief priests and the elders. The traitor had given the crowd a signal: 'The man I kiss is the one you want. Arrest him!'

Judas went straight to Jesus and said, 'Peace be with you, Teacher,' and kissed him. Jesus answered, 'Be quick about it friend!'

Then they came up, arrested Jesus, and held him tight. One of those who were with Jesus drew his sword and

> struck at the High Priest's slave, cutting off his ear. 'Put your sword back in its place,' Jesus said to him. 'All who take the sword will die by the sword. Don't you know that I could call on my father for help, and at once he would send me more than twelve armies of angels?'

Story

In 1995 a Christian Brother, Br. Senan Kerrigan, was brutally murdered in Sierra Leone. Below are extracts from a statement made by Br. L. Gillespie on behalf of the Christian Brothers in that area.

> 'We accept unconditionally from God the gift of Br. Senan's life and death. We forgive those who shot him. We forgive those who divided his possessions among them, and those who mocked him. We pray for them especially, we seek to blame no one nor do we condone the evil that slay the innocent.
>
> We are aware that Br. Senan is only one of thousands of innocent men and women who have met apparently random violent deaths on the roads and in the villages of Sierra Leone in the last few years. These violent deaths of good, innocent men and women continue on a daily basis. If Senan's death cries out on behalf of the voiceless victims it may be one more seed for a new peaceful world. We hope that in some way his death and the awareness that it creates, will help minds and hearts to become attuned to the divine energy for love and peace in the world...
>
> We miss him greatly.'

Activity

Ask pupils to write a letter to someone with whom they are angry or would wish revenge. In the letter pupils should try to express some understanding of the point of view of the other person and might suggest a peaceful solution to the problem.

Prayer

This prayer was found scribbled on a piece of wrapping paper near the body of a dead child at Ravensbruck concentration camp:

O Lord, remember not only the men and women of good will but also those of evil will. But do not remember all the suffering they have inflicted upon us; remember the fruits we have borne thanks to this suffering...

Our comradeship, our loyalty, our humility, our courage, our generosity, the greatness of heart which has grown out of all this; and when they come to the judgement, let all the fruits that we have borne be their forgiveness.

7 • Possessions

Introduction

Sometimes our possessions or money come first in our lives. Christians believe that there is a great danger of putting material things before God or other people. In the reading from Mark's Gospel, Jesus points out to the Rich Young Man that his love of money prevents him from finding true happiness and from entering the Kingdom of God.

Scripture

The reading is from *Mark 10:17–23*.

Jesus was starting on his way again, a man ran up, knelt before him, and asked him, 'Good Teacher, what must I do to receive eternal life?'

'Why do you call me good?' Jesus asked him. 'No one is good except God alone. You know the commandments: "Do not commit murder; do not commit adultery; do not steal; do not accuse anyone falsely; do not cheat; respect your father and your mother."'

'Teacher,' the man said, 'ever since I was young, I have obeyed all these commandments.' Jesus looked straight at him with love and said, 'You need only one thing. Go and sell all you have and give the money to the poor, and you will have riches in heaven; then come and follow me.'

When the man heard this, gloom spread over his face, and he went away sad, because he was very rich.

Jesus looked around at his disciples and said to them,

'How hard it will be for rich people to enter the Kingdom of God!'

Story

This account of how people catch monkeys in India can be compared to how we can feel trapped by the possessions, ambitions or way of life that we hold on to.

There is a sure method of catching monkeys that involves putting a nut or scrap of food in a small box. The box has a hole cut in it that is large enough for a monkey to reach into. When the monkey grabs the food his clenched hand is now too large to be withdrawn from the box. The monkey then has a choice, to let go of the nut and keep his freedom or to keep hold and remain trapped. Most monkeys keep hold of their new-found treasure and are later picked up by the hunters.

Activity

For discussion/reflection:

The rich young man was unable to give up all that he possessed. Pupils should consider what possession they would find most difficult to give up and why.

Prayer

We pray that when we treasure each of our possessions, we consider those who have nothing; and when we hold onto all that we own we understand that our belongings may serve to trap us.

8 • The poor

Introduction

When we feel hungry often our instant reaction is to have something to eat. When we see pictures of the poor and starving often our reaction is to turn away. We can feel guilty, unsure of how we can help.

It is one of the roles of charities such as OXFAM, Christian Aid and CAFOD to provide a link with those people who need help and those who want to help. If the activity is to take place you could tell pupils that this week they will have an opportunity to help in a very practical way by going without food and donating the money saved to the poor.

However, in helping this way not only will they be giving money to those who need it but they will also grow a little in understanding of what it feels to be hungry.

Scripture

In the miracle of the feeding of the 5,000. Jesus made sure that each person had enough to eat. Christians believe we have the responsibility to share what we have with the poor.

> Jesus asked the Disciples, 'How much bread have you got? Go and see.'
>
> When they found out, they told him, 'Five loaves and also two fish.'
>
> Jesus then told his disciples to make all the people divide into groups and sit down on the green grass. So

the people sat down in rows, in groups of a hundred and groups of fifty. Then Jesus took the five loaves and the two fish, looked up to heaven, and gave thanks to God. He broke the loaves and gave them to his disciples to distribute to the people. He also divided the two fish among them all. Everyone ate and had enough. Then the disciples took up twelve baskets full of what was left of the bread and the fish. The number of men who were fed was five thousand.

Story

This account is written by the newsreader Michael Buerk at the time of the Ethiopian famine.

I'll never forget the day that I found out what desperate hunger is really like for so many millions of people, who live on the very borders of existence.

My camera team and I had been filming the results of the Ethiopian famine. We had spent several days watching people die in front of us, children as well as adults, and seen tens of thousands of poor Ethiopians who did not seem far away from that fate. We were, I realise now, in a mild state of shock. So much horror around; such an enormous scale of suffering. It was a paradox of this famine that when we went into a village in the middle of the worst affected area we found a cafe of sorts that was not only open but sold Coca-Cola and bread rolls. We sat in the corner of this mud room and were able to have these things for breakfast when there was a commotion at the door.

There must have been several hundred starving people fighting for a chance to see somebody eating. At the very front was an old man, lined and wiry. His eyes were wide and his hands were trembling. He fell to his knees and, very slowly, started to move towards us across the floor with both hands stretched out, begging, in front on him.

Who could have eaten under those circumstances? But what could we do? We gave the old man some bread and went out into the street and, in a pathetic sort of way, tried to break up the rolls to feed all those people.

I have never felt so useless and I'm sure my colleagues felt the same. There was really nothing any of us could say to each other for some time after.

Activity

Pupils should be encouraged to try and go without something that they would usually have: a packet of crisps or a drink, or a bar of chocolate. As a class the money that would have been spent could be collected and given to one of the aid charities. A representative of one of the charities could be invited to talk at a year group or whole-school assembly.

Prayer

The following Christian prayer speaks of our reluctance to get 'too involved'.

You asked for my hands
that you might use them for your purposes.
I gave them for a moment; then withdrew
them, for
the work was hard.

You asked for my mouth
to speak out against injustice.
I gave you a whisper that I might not be
accused.

You asked for my eyes
to see the pain of poverty.
I closed them, for I did not want to see.

You asked for my life
that you might work through me
I gave you a small part that I might not get
'too involved'.

Lord, forgive me for calculated efforts to
serve you
only when it is convenient to do so,
only in those places where it is safe to do so,
and
only with those who make it easy to do so.

Father, forgive me, renew me,
send me out as a usable instrument,
that I might take seriously the meaning of your cross.

9 • Success

Introduction

> 'That man is a success who has lived well, laughed often,
>   and loved much;
> who has gained the respect of intelligent men and the love
>   of children;
> who has fulfilled his niche and accomplished his task;
> who leaves the world better than he found it, whether by
>   an improved poppy,
> a perfect poem or a rescued soul, who never lacked
>   appreciation of Earth's beauty,
> or failed to express it; who looked for the best in others
>   and gave the best he had;
> his memory is a benediction.'
>
> (R.L. STEVENSON)

It seems to be a basic human need to achieve success in life. Success, though, is judged in many different ways. Those who have achieved greatness or fame or who have amassed wealth and power, these may be considered to be successful people.

However, the words of Stevenson and Martin Luther King point to another measure of a successful life: for them, to have loved much is to be a success.

Scripture

In the reading from *Mark 9:33–38*, the disciples were arguing about greatness, about success. In reply, Jesus expressed what he believed true success to be.

> They came to Capernaum, and after going indoors Jesus asked his disciples, 'What were you arguing about on the road?' But they would not answer him, because on the road they had been arguing among themselves about who was the greatest. Jesus sat down, called the twelve disciples, and said to them, 'Whoever wants to be first must place himself last of all and be servant of all.' Then he took a child and made him stand in front of them. He put his arms around him and said to them, 'Whoever welcomes in my name one of these children, welcomes me; and whoever welcomes me, welcomes not only me but the one who sent me.'

Story

> 'Every now and then,' he told the congregation, 'I think about my own death'. His words brought a low murmur of surprise from the parishioners.
>
> 'I don't think of it in a morbid sense,' he qualified, smiling faintly. 'I ask myself what would I want said. If any of you are around when I have to meet my day...I don't want a long funeral. And tell them not to mention that I have a Nobel Peace Prize. Tell them not to mention where I went to school. None of that is important. I'd like somebody to mention that day that...Martin Luther King, Jr., tried to give his life for serving others...I'd like somebody to mention that day that...Martin Luther King tried to love somebody...
>
> I want you to be able to say that day that...I did try to feed the hungry...that I did try in my life to clothe those who were naked...that I did try in my life to visit those who were in prison...
>
> All the other shallow things will not matter. I won't have any money to leave behind. I won't have the fine

and luxurious things of life to leave behind. But I just want to leave a committed life behind.

That's all I want to say. If I can help somebody as I pass along...if I can cheer somebody with a word or song...if I can show somebody that he's travelling wrong...then my living will not be in vain.

If I can do my duty as a Christian ought...if I can spread the message as the Master taught...then my living will not be in vain.

(MARTIN LUTHER KING)

Activity

Pupils should be reminded about the definitions of a eulogy and an obituary. Examples from newspapers of obituaries would help to reinforce the idea. In addition, if available, a clip from the funeral scene of the film *Four Weddings and a Funeral* would provide a powerful example of a eulogy. Pupils should then be given time to reflect on the following questions and to discuss the responses in small groups.

At your funeral what would you want said?

What would you want to be remembered for?

Write an obituary or a eulogy about yourself.

Prayer

We pray that in our lives we may understand the meaning of success, we may strive for true greatness and may learn to live as a servant of others.

10 • Hope

Introduction

Of all the insults that we could throw at one another, to be called 'hopeless' is perhaps one of the worst. To be called hopeless comments on how you are now but also says that there is no chance of improving. Two famous people who were labelled hopeless in school were Sir Winston Churchill, who went on to be a real inspiration of hope to people throughout World War II, and Albert Einstein. Einstein was told at school that 'nothing good would ever come of him'. He proved to be one of the greatest scientists the world has ever known.

Of course *nobody* is hopeless but the sort of hope that Churchill and Einstein showed was not a hope linked to dreams and wishes, not the sort of hope we have when we do the lottery or when we want the team that we support to win – their hope was a combination of belief and determination.

Scripture

The reading is from *Mark 7:24–30*. Jesus tests the woman to see if she has enough faith. He tells her that He would only heal Jews ('the children') not gentiles (non-Jews). The woman's answer proves both her belief and her determination.

> Jesus went away to the territory near the city of Tyre. He went into a house and did not want anyone to know he was there. A woman whose daughter had an evil spirit in her, heard about Jesus and came to him at once and fell at his feet. The woman was a gentile. She begged Jesus to

drive the demon out of her daughter. But Jesus answered, 'let us first feed the children. It isn't right to take the children's food and throw it to the dogs.'

'Sir,' she answered, 'even the dogs under the table eat the children's left-overs!' So Jesus said to her, 'Because of that answer, go back home, where you will find that the demon has gone back out of your daughter!'

She went home and found her child lying on the bed; her daughter was well!

Story

Two frogs fell into a bucket of cream. They tried hard to get out by climbing up the side of the bucket. But each time they slipped back again.

Finally one frog said: 'We'll never get out of here. I give up.' So down he went and drowned. The other frog decided to keep trying. So again and again he tried to climb with his front legs and he kicked with his back legs. Suddenly he hit something hard. He turned to see what it was and discovered that all his kicking had churned up a lump of butter! He hopped on top of it and leaped out to safety.

Activity

Pupils should be encouraged to reflect on and discuss the following questions.

What are *your* hopes for

- yourself
- your family and friends
- the world?

Prayer

When we are discouraged, when we feel that there is no hope, we pray to have the belief and determination to carry on.

11 • Vision

Introduction

> 'Pussycat, pussycat, where have you been?
> I've been to London to look at the Queen.
> Pussycat, pussycat, what did you do there?
> I saw a little mouse under her chair.'

Have you ever thought of whether the pussycat *could* have commented on the splendour and riches of Buckingham Palace or on the thrill or honour of meeting the Queen? No, the only thing that was of significance to the cat was a little mouse – the cat was only able to see what was important to him.

Often what happens in our lives is dependent on our own view of the world, our own vision of life. Some people may see life as full of optimism and opportunity and will view people as generally good. Others may see the world as a dark and foreboding place and will view people with suspicion and mistrust. Sometimes we will only see what we want to see in people and in the world. But then, like the pussycat, we may miss a great deal.

Scripture

The reading is from *Matthew 5:3–12*. In the Sermon on the Mount Jesus outlines the basic Christian vision of life.

> Happy are those who know they are spiritually poor; the
> Kingdom of Heaven belongs to them!

Happy are those who mourn; God will comfort them!

Happy are those who are humble; they will receive what God has promised!

Happy are those whose greatest desire is to do what God requires; God will satisfy them fully!

Happy are those who are merciful to others; God will be merciful to them!

Happy are the pure in heart; they will see God!

Happy are those who work for peace; God will call them his children!

Happy are those who are persecuted because they do what God requires; the Kingdom of Heaven belongs to them!

Happy are you when people insult you and persecute you and tell all kinds of evil lies against you because you are my followers. Be happy and glad, for a great reward is kept for you in heaven.

Story

A traveller met a wise man on the road linking two towns. They were travelling in opposite directions.

'Tell me about the town ahead', the traveller asked, 'Are the people friendly, will I be welcomed there?'

The wise man paused, 'Tell me about the town you have come from', he replied.

'The town was an ugly place and I was glad to leave. It was full of wicked, unfriendly people who made no effort to welcome strangers.'

'Then', said the wise man, 'You will find the town ahead to be exactly the same'.

Activity

Pupils should complete the following.
- I think the world is...
- Life is...
- People are...

Prayer

We pray that we learn to see the world not with suspicion and mistrust but with a renewed vision of hope and optimism.

12 • Understanding

Introduction

There is an old American Indian proverb that you should not judge a person until you have walked a mile in his moccasins. In other words we should not judge someone until we have made real attempts to understand them. We all wish to be understood, we all wish that people could see life as we see it. The poem 'What do you see nurses...' was written by Kate who spent the end of her life in a hospital. She could not speak and nurses had no idea of her feelings until the poem was discovered in her locker after her death.

Scripture

The reading from John shows the compassion and understanding of Jesus for the adulterous woman.

At dawn he appeared again in the temple courts, where all the people gathered round him, and he sat down to teach them.

The teachers of the law and the Pharisees brought in a woman caught in adultery. They made her stand before the group, and said to Jesus, 'Teacher, this woman was caught in the act of adultery. In the Law Moses commanded us to stone such women. Now what do you say?' They were using this question as a trap, in order to have a basis for accusing him. But Jesus bent down and started to write on the ground with his finger. When they kept on questioning him, he straightened up and said to them, 'If any one of you is without sin, let him be the first to throw a stone at her.' Again he stooped down and wrote on the ground. At this, those who heard began to go away one at a time, the older ones first, until only Jesus was left, with the woman still standing there.

Jesus straightened up and asked her, 'Woman, where are they? Has no-one condemned you?'

'No-one sir,' she said. 'Then neither do I condemn you,' Jesus declared. 'Go now and leave your life of sin.'

Story

What do you see nurses, what do you see?
Are you thinking, when you're looking at me:
A crabbit old woman, not very wise,
Uncertain of habit with far-away eyes,
Who dribbles her food and makes no reply,
When you say in a loud voice 'I do wish you'd try'
I'll tell you who I am as I sit here so still,
As I rise at your bidding, as I eat at your will.
I'm a small child of ten with a father and mother,
Brothers and sisters who love one another.
A bride soon at twenty, my heart gives a leap,
remembering the vows I promised to keep.
At twenty-five now I have young of my own,
Who need me to build a secure, happy home.
At fifty once more babies play round my knee,
Again we know children my loved one and me.
Dark days are upon me, my husband is dead,
I look to the future, I shudder with dread.
For my young are all busy rearing young of their own,
I think of the years and the love I have known.
I'm an old woman now, but nature is cruel,
'Tis her jest to make old age look like a fool.
The body it crumbles, grace and vigour depart,
There is now a stone, where I once had a heart,
But inside this old carcase, a young girl still dwells,

And now and again my battered heart swells.
I remember the joys, I remember the pain,
And I'm loving and living life over again.
I think of the years all too few – gone too fast,
And accept the stark fact that nothing will last.
So open your eyes nurse, open and see,
Not a crabbit old woman, look closer see ME.

Activity

Pupils should write a poem in the style of Kate's poem. It could be addressed to parents, friends, teachers or whoever they choose. It should begin with the lines:

'What do you see (teachers), what do you see,
What do you see when you're looking at me?'

Prayer

From the prayer of Francis, a Christian saint

Lord...grant that I may try
not to be comforted but to comfort
not to be understood but to understand
not to be loved but to love.
Because it is in giving that we receive,
It is in forgiving that we are forgiven
and it is in dying that we are born to eternal life.

13 • Thanksgiving

Introduction

When Superman actor Christopher Reeve played the part of a sports star who was crippled by injury he spoke of the horror of losing all that you take for granted. It was a tragic irony that some months after his latest film had been made, Reeve was himself paralysed in a riding accident. The man who played Superman was now unable to walk.

There is a saying that you never really appreciate something until you are in danger of losing it. We are probably all guilty of taking things and people for granted. Therefore, now and again it is important to be thankful for all that we have, for we may not always have it.

Scripture

The reading is from *Luke 17:11–19*. In this well-known reading we hear that only one leper returned to give thanks for being healed.

As Jesus made his way to Jerusalem, he went along the border between Samaria and Galilee. He was going into a village when he was met by ten men suffering from a dreaded skin disease. They stood at a distance and shouted, 'Jesus! Master! Take pity on us!' Jesus saw them and said to them, 'Go and let the priests examine you.'

On the way they were made clean. When one of them saw that he was healed, he came back, praising God in a loud voice. He threw himself to the ground at Jesus' feet and thanked him. The man was a Samaritan. Jesus said, 'There were ten men who were healed; where are the other nine? Why is this foreigner the only one who came back to give thanks to God?' And Jesus said to him, 'Get up and go; your faith has made you well.'

Story

A farmer was fed up with his life. He was surrounded by noise and mess. He constantly shouted at his wife, his wife shouted at him and they both shouted at the children. He went to the wise man of the village for advice. 'Take one of your sheep and let it live in the front room', suggested the wise man. The farmer did as he was told.

A month later the man returned – his life was terrible! The sheep caused chaos, it ate the furniture and left a mess everywhere. The farmer told the wise man that he could not go on.

'Take one of your prize cows,' the wise man said, 'and keep it in the kitchen.' The farmer did as he was told.

A month later the man returned, his life was now completely unbearable. The sheep had eaten all the carpets, the cow had destroyed the kitchen, the smell was hideous, the mess indescribable. The whole family screamed at each other day and night. They just could not go on any longer.

'Sell your sheep and the cow', the wise man suggested. The farmer did as he was told. A month later the farmer returned – his life was bliss! The house was clean and quiet, the farmer talked to his wife, his wife talked to him, and they both talked to the children'.

'I've got a lot to be thankful for', the farmer said.

'Yes!' said the wise man.

Activity

'You never really appreciate something until you are in danger of losing it.'

Ask pupils to suggest what *three* things they would miss if they were taken away from them. Giving thanks for these things could form part of a prayer.

Prayer

We often pray for our needs and wishes. This week we pray in thanks for the everyday things that we take for granted; for freedom, for health, for friendship. We also remember this week those who are deprived of these essential features of life.

14 • Imprisoned

Introduction

Throughout the world there are many people who have been imprisoned, tortured or killed because of their beliefs. Often they are not given a fair trial or dealt with in a just or fair way.

One particular charity, Amnesty International, campaigns to support such prisoners and aims to encourage all aspects of Human Rights. Members write short and respectful letters to heads of governments, justice ministers or the appropriate authority. The letter requests the immediate and unconditional release of a prisoner of conscience, an end to torture or a halt to an execution. Often prisoners are released or treated more humanely as a result of the pressure from the members of Amnesty International.

Christians believe that they should follow the example of Christ and strive for justice. The work of Amnesty International is one way of helping to create a more just and peaceful world.

Scripture

The reading from *Isaiah 61:1–4* speaks of bringing good news to the poor, lonely and imprisoned.

> He has chosen me and sent me
> to bring good news to the poor,
> To heal the broken-hearted,
> to announce release to captives,
> and freedom to those in prison.
> He has sent me to proclaim,
> that the time has come

when the Lord will save his people,
and defeat their enemies.
He has sent me to comfort all who
mourn in Zion,
Joy and gladness instead of grief,
a song of praise instead of sorrow.
They will be like trees
that the Lord himself has planted.
They will all do what is right,
and God will be praised for what he
has done.
They will rebuild cities that have
long been in ruin.

Story

'I'll tell you a small story which I told in Damascus. I was kept in total and complete isolation for four years. I saw no one and spoke to no one.

One day, out of the blue, a guard came with a postcard. It was a postcard showing a stained-glass window from Bedford showing John Bunyan in jail.

And I looked at that card and I thought, "My word Bunyan you're a lucky fellow. You've got a window out of which you can look, see the sky and here I am in a dark room. You've got pen and ink, you can write but here I am, I've got nothing and you've got your own clothes and a table and a chair."

And I turned the card over and there was a message from someone whom I don't know simply saying, "We remember, we shall not forget. We shall continue to pray for you and to work for all people who are detained around the world."

That thought sent me back to the marvellous work of agencies like Amnesty International and their letter-writing campaigns and I would say never despise those simple actions. Something, somewhere, will get through to the people you are concerned about as it got through to me and to my fellows eventually.'

(TERRY WAITE, 19 NOVEMBER 1991)

Activity

Further details of the work of Amnesty International can be obtained from:

Amnesty International – British Section
93–119 Rosebery Avenue,
London EC1R 4RE
Tel: 0171 278 6000

Pupils could be encouraged to write to a particular prisoner of conscience or to support the work of the charity through membership or donations.

Prayer

We pray for all those who suffer injustice in the world, those who are imprisoned, tortured or killed. We pray also for those who inflict injustice, that their hearts may be changed through the work and commitment of charities such as Amnesty International.

15 • Sharing

Introduction

From a very early age we are taught to share. At that age we may understand it as sharing our sweets, or sharing our time. Real sharing goes deeper than that – it means to understand others, to share their feelings, their thoughts, their desires: to laugh with the happy, to cry with the sad, to understand the angry, and to be with the lonely. Real sharing means realising that we are all part of the one family, all part of the same humanity.

Scripture

The reading is from St. Paul's first letter to the Corinthians (12:21–26). In these few lines St. Paul points out that we are all responsible for one another, we all share in each other's sadnesses and we share in each other's joys.

> We cannot do without the parts of the body that seem to be weaker; and those parts that we think aren't worth very much are the ones which we treat with greater care; while the parts of the body which don't look very nice are treated with special modesty, which the more beautiful parts do not need. God himself has put the body together in such a way as to give greater honour to those parts that need it. And so there is no division in the body, but all its different parts have the same concern for one another. If one part of the body suffers, all the other parts suffer with it; if one part is praised, all the other parts share its happiness.

Story

> If you think blows struck in Ireland won't hurt you –
> think again – they will hurt you.
>
> If you think the knife slid between the ribs of a Pakistani
> will glance off your skin –
> think again – it will hurt you.
>
> If you think bullets hissing towards beating hearts in some
> country we know nothing about will miss you –
> think again – it will not miss your beating heart.
>
> If you think needles jabbed into the veins to make the
> blood run docile won't prick you –
> think again – they will hurt you, hit you, prick you –
> and they will not miss you.
>
> We are all one.

Activity

Ask pupils to look through a selection of recent newspapers and to identify stories about people who have suffered violence, sadness or loneliness.

Ask them to discuss the following.

Do these stories affect each one of us?

How can we respond?

Prayer

> We have all been created equal in dignity, equal in the need for respect, love and care. We pray that we can learn to share the riches that we have been given, with those who are deprived of dignity and love.

16 • Seize the day

Introduction

In the film *Dead Poet's Society*, Robin Williams plays the role of an inspirational teacher. He uses the Latin phrase *carpe diem*, or 'seize the day', to try to motivate his pupils. To seize the day means not to be involved with sentimental memories of the past or of unrealistic dreams of the future but to see every second as precious. To seize the day is to live out your past, future and present in each moment of each day.

Scripture

The reading from *Luke* tells of a man who did not seize the day but spent his time storing up riches for the future.

And he told them this parable: 'The ground of a certain rich man produced a good crop. He thought to himself, "What shall I do? I have no place to store my crops." Then he said, "This is what I'll do. I will tear down my barns and build bigger ones, and there I will store all my grain and my goods. And I'll say to myself, 'You have plenty of good things laid up for many years. Take life easy; eat, drink and be merry."

But God said to him, "You fool! This very night your life will be demanded from you. Then who will get what you have prepared for yourself?" This is how it will be with anyone who stores up things for himself but is not rich towards God.'

Then Jesus said to his disciples: 'Therefore I tell you, do

not worry about your life, what you will eat; or about your body, what you will wear. Life is more than food, and the body more than clothes. Consider the ravens: They do not sow or reap, they have no storeroom or barn; yet God feeds them. And how much more valuable you are than birds! Who of you by worrying can add a single hour to his life? Since you cannot do this very little thing, why do you worry about the rest?'

Story

Look to this day, for it is life, the very life of life.
In its brief course lie all the realities and truth of existence –
the joy of growth, the splendour of action, the glory of power.
For yesterday is but a memory, and tomorrow is only a vision,
But today well lived makes every yesterday a memory of happiness,
and every tomorrow a vision of hope.
Look well, therefore to this day.

(SANSKRIT POEM)

Activity

There is an old saying that you should not put off until tomorrow what you can do today.

Pupils should list three things that are their realistic dreams of the future.

What can be done *today* to begin to make the dreams a reality?

Prayer

We have been given this day.
We pray that it is a day well lived.

17 • Get a life

Introduction

'Fab', 'hip', 'trendy', 'relax, man'. Many words or phrases are specific to certain times or trends. Out of context they seem silly and dated. A phrase of the present time seems to be 'Get a life!' But what does it mean to get a life? Is it to do with success, achievement, possessions or money? Is it to do with image, popularity, doing what everyone else is doing?

Many stories in the Bible talk about the people gaining a new life. This new life often means letting go of the things that people allow to dominate their lives, such as power, money, or possessions. In letting go of these, space is given for others and for God.

Scripture

The reading is from *Genesis 12:1–4*. In this story God has called Abram to a new life. Abram was seventy-five years old yet he was to give up all he had known to follow the word of God. A sign of his new life was Abram's new name, Abraham, the 'father of all nations'.

> The Lord said to Abram, 'Leave your native land, your relatives, and your father's home and go to a country that I am going to show you. I will give you many descendants, and they will become a great nation. I will bless you and make your name famous, so that you will be a blessing.
> I will bless those who bless you,
> but I will curse those who curse you.
> And through you I will bless all the nations.'

Story

Once upon a time there was an old man from the lovely island of Crete. He loved his land with a deep and beautiful intensity, so much so that when he perceived that he was about to die he had his sons bring him outside and lay him on his beloved earth. As he was about to expire he reached down by his side and clutched some earth into his hands. He died a happy man.

He now appeared before heaven's gates. God, as an old white bearded man, came out to greet him. 'Welcome,' he said. 'You've been a good man. Please come into the joys of heaven.' But as the old man started to enter the pearly gates, God said, 'Please. You must let the soil go.' 'Never!' said the old man stepping back. 'Never!' And so God departed sadly, leaving the old man outside the gates. A few aeons went by. God came out again, this time as an old drinking friend. They had a few drinks, told some stories, and then God said, 'All right, now it's time to enter heaven, friend. Let's go.' And they started for the pearly gates. And once more God requested that the old man let go of this soil and once more he refused.

More aeons rolled by. God came out once more, this time as a delightful and playful granddaughter. 'Oh, granddaddy,' she said, "you're so wonderful and we all miss you. Please come inside with me.' The old man nodded and she helped him up for by this time he had grown very old and arthritic indeed. In fact so arthritic was he that he had to prop up the right hand holding Crete's soil with his left hand. They moved towards the pearly gates and at this point his strength quite gave out. His gnarled fingers would no longer stay clenched in a fist with the result that the soil sifted out between them until his hand was empty. He then entered heaven.

The first thing he saw was his beloved island.

Activity

A 'haiku' is a three-line poem with a sharp or surprising ending. It has seventeen syllables arranged in three lines of five, seven and five syllables. Ask pupils to write a haiku on the theme 'Get a life'. An example is given below:

Friends say, 'Act like me!'
'You don't fit', 'Change your image'
Whose life? Mine or yours?

Prayer

We pray that we come to understand what it means to be fully human and that we will strive to live our lives in a new way.

18 • Lamed Vovnik

Introduction

There is an old Jewish tradition or legend that says the world continues to exist because of the presence of 36 good, just and heroic people. These 36 are known as *Lamed Vovnik*. Today, and throughout history, the world will always be a better place because of the true heroes of life.

Scripture

David was a great King and hero for the Jews. In the story from *1 Samuel* we hear of the boy David slaying Goliath (the Philistine).

> Meanwhile, the Philistine, with his shield-bearer in front of him, kept coming closer to David.
>
> He looked David over and saw that he was only a boy, ruddy and handsome, and he despised him. He said to David, 'Am I a dog, that you come at me with sticks?' And the Philistine cursed David by his gods.
>
> 'Come here,' he said, 'and I'll give your flesh to the birds of the air and the beasts of the field!'
>
> David said to the Philistine, 'You come against me with sword and spear and javelin, but I come against you in the name of the Lord Almighty, the God of the armies of Israel, whom you have defied. This day the Lord will hand you over to me, and I'll strike you down and cut off your head. Today I will give the carcasses of the Philistine army to the birds of the air and the beasts of the earth, and the whole world will know that there is a God in Israel. All

those gathered here will know that it is not by sword or spear that the Lord saves; for the battle is the Lord's, and he will give all of you into our hands.'

As the Philistine moved closer to attack him, David ran quickly towards the battle line to meet him. Reaching into his bag and taking out a stone, he slung it and struck the Philistine on the forehead. The stone sank into his forehead, and he fell face down on the ground.

So David triumphed over the Philistine with a sling and a stone; without a sword in his hand he struck down the Philistine and killed him.

Story

The film *Schindler's List* tells the story of Oskar Schindler, a Czechoslovakian businessman. At the start of the war Schindler exploited the Nazi occupation of Poland and Czechoslovakia. He used Jews who had been taken by the Germans as free sources of slave labour. However in the film we see the slow transformation of Oskar Schindler from a manipulative and selfish factory owner to a man who was prepared to risk all that he had to save the lives of innocent Jews.

In the moving, final scenes of the film Itzhak Stern, Schindler's assistant, presents him with a ring on behalf of all the Jews whose lives had been spared. The ring was in recognition of the great heroism and bravery of Schindler. Inscribed inside the ring were the words 'Whoever saves one life, saves the world entire'.

Today, due to the mass extermination of Jews by the Nazis, there are less than 4,000 Jews in Poland. Descendants of 'Schindler's Jews' total more than 6,000.

Activity

Whoever saves one life, saves the world entire'.

Ask pupils to reflect on this statement and then to give examples of people who have shown great heroism. Pupils could be encouraged to look through newspapers and magazines and arrange a display of clippings showing various acts of heroism, goodness or selflessness.

Prayer

'First they came for the Jews and I did not speak out – because I was not a Jew.

Then they came for the communists and I did not speak out – because I was not a communist.

Then they came for the trade unionists and I did not speak out – because I was not a trade unionist.

Then they came for me and there was no one left to speak out for me'

(WRITTEN BY A VICTIM OF THE NAZIS).

We pray in thanks for those who have spoken out, for the people who, in many different ways, are good, just or heroic.

19 • Influence

Introduction

When a stone is dropped onto water, the ripples will spread far and wide. The initial action of dropping the stone has its effect a great distance away. In a similar way the actions that we take can have a tremendous effect on others. We have a huge capacity to influence others for good or for bad.

In the film *It's a Wonderful Life*, James Stewart plays the role of George Bailey. Bailey is given the opportunity to see what the world would have been like if he had never been born. He realises that not only has he influenced and affected those close to him but people that he had never met had benefited because he had lived. George Bailey realises that one good action, like the ripples on a pond, can spread far and wide.

Scripture

The reading is from *Mark 4*. In the parable of the Sower, Jesus explains how, although people may hear God's message many will be influenced by worries and problems or riches and desires. Only a few will be truly influenced by His message.

> 'Listen! Once there was a man who went out to sow corn. As he scattered the seed in the field, some of it fell along the path, and the birds came and ate it up. Some of it fell on rocky ground where there was little soil. The seeds soon sprouted because the roots were not deep. Then when the sun came up it burnt the young plants; and because the roots had not grown deep enough, the plants

soon dried up. Some of the seed fell among thorn bushes, which grew up and choked the plants, and they didn't produce any corn. But, some seeds fell on good soil, and the plants sprouted, grew, and produced corn; some had thirty grains, others sixty, and others a hundred...' Then Jesus asked them, 'Don't you understand this parable? How then will you understand any parable? The sower sows God's message. Some people are like the seeds that fall along the path; as soon as they hear the message, Satan comes along and takes it away. Other people are like the seeds that fall on rocky ground. As soon as they receive the message they receive it gladly. But it does not sink deep into them, and they don't last long. So once trouble or persecution comes because of the message, they give up at once. Others are like the seeds sown among the thorn bushes. These are the ones who hear the message, but the worries about this life, the love for riches and all other kinds of desires crowd in and choke the message, and they don't bear fruit. But other people are like the seeds sown in good soil. They hear the message, accept it, and bear fruit: some thirty, some sixty, and some a hundred.'

Story

Ernest Gordon (who wrote *Miracle on the River Kwai*) tells of the amazing change that took place in a Japanese prisoner-of-war camp in Burma between Christmas 1942 and Christmas 1943. In 1942 the camp was a sea of mud and filth. It was a scene of sweated labour and brutal treatment by the Japanese guards. There was hardly any food, and everyone looked only after himself. Twelve months later, the ground of the camp was cleared and clean. Huts had been rebuilt and on Christmas morning 2,000 men were at worship. What had happened?

During the year one prisoner had shared his last crumb of food with another man who was also in desperate need. Then he had died. Amongst his belongings they found a Bible. Could this be the secret of his life, of his willingness to give to others and not to grasp for himself? One by one the prisoners began to read it. Soon the Spirit of God began to grip their hearts and change their lives.

Both the actions and beliefs of that man had enormous impact on the lives of many others.

Activity

Pupils should think about one recent good action of theirs and one recent bad action. Each of these actions should form the centre of a spider diagram. Radiating from each of the actions they should indicate some of the consequences, both known and imagined. Can further lines be drawn to indicate the next level of consequences?

Prayer

We pray in thanks for all those who have a positive influence on us.

We ask that all our actions and words serve only to better our world.

20 • Faith

Introduction

In the book *Children's Letters to God* the last letter is written by Eugene. He writes, 'I didn't think orange went very good with purple until I saw the sunset you made on Tue. That was cool.'

Often we cannot make sense of what we see in our world – the wars, the cruelty, the anger and the neglect. People of faith trust in the presence of God, they believe that there is a meaning and reason to all things. And that one day, like Eugene, they will see the sunset and understand God's plan.

Scripture

The reading from *Mark 10:46–52* tells the story of the healing of Blind Bartimaeus. In this, as in many other miracles, Jesus stresses the importance of faith. The story serves to emphasise that miracles happen as a result of faith and not the other way round.

Then they came to Jericho. As Jesus and his disciples, together with a large crowd, were leaving the city, a blind man, Bartimaeus (that is, the Son of Timaeus), was sitting by the roadside begging. When he heard that it was Jesus of Nazareth, he began to shout, 'Jesus, Son of David, have mercy on me!'

Many rebuked him and told him to be quiet, but he shouted all the more, 'Son of David, have mercy on me!'

Jesus stopped and said, 'Call him.' So they called to the blind man. 'Cheer up! On your feet! He's calling you.'

Throwing his cloak aside, he jumped to his feet and came to Jesus.

'What do you want me to do for you?' Jesus asked him. The blind man said, 'Rabbi, I want to see.'

'Go,' said Jesus, 'your faith has healed you.' Immediately he received his sight and followed Jesus along the road.

Story

'In spite of everything I still believe that people are really good at heart. I simply can't build up my hopes on a foundation consisting of confusion, misery and death. I see the world gradually being turned into a wilderness, I hear the ever approaching thunder, which will destroy us too, I can feel the suffering of millions and yet, if I look up to the heavens, I think that it will all come right, that this cruelty will end, and that peace and tranquillity will return again...I want to go on living after my death. And therefore I am grateful to God for giving me this gift...of expressing all that is in me.'

(FROM THE DIARY OF ANNE FRANK)

Activity

Pupils should draw a timeline, starting at their birth up until the present day. The line should show the ups and downs of their lives. Particular moments of joy or sadness could be marked. On the timeline they could also include occasions when they have experienced particularly strong feelings of belief or disbelief in the presence of God.

Prayer

In moments of great joy and in times of deepest despair we pray for the ability to see sense, meaning and reason in all things.

21 • Wisdom

Introduction

The author John Powell said one of the greatest sadnesses in the world is that we can quickly learn to love things and use people rather than use things and love people. In a busy, competitive world it is easy to get confused about what is important and what is trivial. Perhaps wisdom is being able to recognise truth, being able to know what is important and what is not.

Scripture

In this reading from *Matthew*, Jesus explains that a wise man is someone who knows what is important, someone who builds on solid foundations. For Christians the words and principles of Jesus are the foundations for a good life.

'Therefore everyone who hears these words of mine and puts them into practice is like a wise man who built his house on the rock.

The rain came down, the streams rose, and the winds blew and beat against that house; yet it did not fall, because it had its foundation on the rock.

But everyone who hears these words of mine and does not put them into practice is like a foolish man who built his house on sand.

The rain came down, the streams rose, and the winds blew and beat against that house, and it fell with a great crash.'

Story

This letter was written by the head of an American high school to his staff.

> Dear Teacher,
>
> I am a survivor of a concentration camp.
> My eyes saw what no man should witness:
> gas chambers built by learned engineers;
> children poisoned by educated physicians;
> infants killed by trained nurses;
> women and babies shot and burned
> by high school and college graduates.
> So, I am suspicious of Education.
> My request is: help your students become more human.
> Your efforts must never produce learned monsters,
> skilled psychopaths, educated Eichmanns.
> Reading, writing, arithmetic are important only
> if they serve to make our children more human.

Activity

Ask pupils to complete the following sentences.

The people that are important in my life are...
The things that are important in my life are...
The things I can change in my life are...
The things that I need to accept in my life are...

Prayer

> I pray for the courage to change the things I can,
> the serenity to accept the things I can't,
> and the wisdom to know the difference.

22 • Creation

Introduction

Christians believe that God gave the world to us to look after on God's behalf. In other words we are God's stewards. Like any good steward we must take our responsibilities seriously and care for the world and everything in it.

When we learn to appreciate the beauty and uniqueness of our planet, when we learn to treasure every aspect of the environment then we may become worthy stewards.

Scripture

The reading is from *Genesis 1:26–31*. It tells the story of the creation of humankind and the responsibility it has for the earth.

> Then God said, 'And now we will make human beings; they will be like us and resemble us. They will have power over the fish, the birds and all the animals, domestic and wild, large and small.' So God created human beings, making them to be like himself. He created them male and female, blessed them and said, 'Have many children, so that your descendants will live all over the earth and bring it under their control. I am putting you in charge of the fish, the birds, and all the wild animals. I have provided all kinds of grain and all kinds of fruit for you to eat; but for all the wild animals and for all the birds I have provided grass and leafy plants for food' – and it was done. God looked at everything he had made, and he was very pleased.

Story

These words are taken from a speech of Chief Seattle in the nine-teenth century when Americans wished to buy the land of the Native Indians.

> How can you buy or sell the sky – the warmth of the land? the idea is strange to us. Yet we do not own the freshness of the air or the sparkle of the water. How can you buy them from us?...Every part of this earth is sacred to my people...We know that the white man does not understand our ways. One portion of the land is the same to him as the next...You must teach your children that the ground beneath their feet is the ashes of our grand-fathers...Teach your children...that the earth is our mother...Love it as we've loved it. Care for it as we've cared for it...With all your strength, with all your might, and with all your heart – preserve it for your children and love it as God loves us all...Man did not weave the web of life, he is merely a strand in it. Whatever he does to the web, he does to himself.

Activity

Pupils should reflect on or discuss the following.

'Whatever he does to the web, he does to himself.'

Pupils should consider some of the actions carried out by people 'developing' the world. What are the consequences of these actions for the earth and nature?

Prayer

> We pray in thanks for the beauty of creation, for the mountains, the sea, the animals and for all of humankind. We pray that we learn to see the world as something to be marvelled at and something to be cared for.

23 • Protest

Introduction

> 'I have cherished the ideal of a democratic and free society in which all persons live together in harmony with equal opportunities. It is an ideal which I hope to live for and to achieve. But if needs be, it is an ideal for which I am prepared to die.'
>
> (NELSON MANDELA)

It is easy to give away a pound if we keep ten for ourselves, it is easy to make a protest if our own security and way of life are not at risk. Throughout history, though, there have been people who were prepared to protest about a situation at great personal cost; people, such as Nelson Mandela, now President of South Africa, who have risked their freedom and their lives to make a stand against injustice, a stand for which Mandela was prepared to die.

Scripture

In this reading from *Mark* Jesus confronts the authorities and their petty rules. He is not afraid to do what is right and heal the man despite the fact that it would bring him much criticism from church leaders.

> One Sabbath Jesus was going through the cornfields and as his disciples walked along they began to pick some ears of corn. The Pharisees said to him, 'Look, why are

they doing what is unlawful on the Sabbath?' He answered, 'Have you never read what David did when he and his companions were hungry and in need?' In the days of Abiathar the high priest, he entered the house of God and ate the consecrated bread, which is lawful only for priests to eat. And he also gave some to his companions.' Then he said to them, 'The Sabbath was made for man, not man for the Sabbath. So the Son of Man is Lord even of the Sabbath.'

Another time he went into the synagogue, and a man with a shrivelled hand was there. Some of them were looking for a reason to accuse Jesus, so they watched him closely to see if he would heal him on the Sabbath. Jesus said to the man with the shrivelled hand, 'Stand up in front of everyone.' Then Jesus asked them, 'Which is lawful on the Sabbath: to do good or to do evil, to save life or to kill?' But they remained silent.

Story

You will probably need to introduce this story by telling the pupils who Khrushchev and Stalin were.

When Khrushchev pronounced his famous denunciation of Stalin, someone in the Congress Hall is reported to have said, 'Where were you, Comrade Khrushchev, when all these innocent people were being slaughtered?'

Khrushchev paused, looked around the hall, and said, 'Will the man who said that kindly stand up!'

Tension mounted in the hall. No one moved. Then Khrushchev said, 'Well, whoever you are, you have your answer now. I was in exactly the same position then as you are now.'

Activity

Ask pupils to think of an issue that is important to them. They should then write a one- minute speech of protest to be delivered to Parliament.

Prayer

We pray that we become people who have the compassion to comfort the disturbed and the courage to disturb the comfortable.

24 • Courage

Introduction

> 'At some ideas you stand perplexed, especially at the sight of human sin, asking yourself whether to combat it by force or by humble love. Always decide, "I will combat it by humble love." If you make up your mind about that once and for all, you may be able to conquer the whole world. Loving humility is a terrible force; the strongest of all and there is nothing like it.'
>
> (DOSTOYEVSKY, *THE BROTHERS KARAMAZOV*)

There are times in all of our lives when we need courage. Sometimes it is the courage to decide to respond with love rather than force. In the story we hear of the tremendous courage of Gordon Wilson. On that November morning he made the decision to combat violence through love. Many people consider the Enniskillen bombings to be a key turning point in the history of conflict in Northern Ireland. The courageous reaction of Gordon Wilson in the face of the horror of the bombings was a genuine symbol of humble love.

Scripture

The reading from *Luke 23* tells of the last moments of Jesus on the cross. Even in his pain and agony Jesus asked for the forgiveness of others.

When they came to the place called the Skull, there they crucified him, along with the criminals – one on his right, the other on his left. Jesus said, 'Father, forgive them, for they do not know what they are doing.' And they divided up his clothes by casting lots.

The people stood watching, and the rulers even sneered at him. They said, 'He saved others; let him save himself if he is the Christ of God, the Chosen One.' The soldiers also came up and mocked him. They offered him wine vinegar and said, 'If you are the king of the Jews, save yourself.'

There was a written notice above him which read: *This is the King of the Jews.* One of the criminals who hung there hurled insults at him: 'Aren't you the Christ? Save yourself and us!' But the other criminal rebuked him. 'Don't you fear God,' he said, 'since you are under the same sentence? We are punished justly, for we are getting what our deeds deserve. But this man has done nothing wrong.' Then he said, 'Jesus, remember me when you come into your kingdom.' Jesus answered him, 'I tell you the truth, today you will be with me in paradise.'

Story

On 11 November 1987 an IRA bomb shattered the peace and the lives of the town of Enniskillen. The people were gathered together on Remembrance Day, amongst them Gordon Wilson and his daughter, Marie. Wilson survived, his daughter, buried in the devastation and rubble, did not. The last words of Marie to her father were: 'Daddy I love you very much'.

Although she had died in his arms in such a brutal and tragic way, Wilson was able to forgive the killers of his daughter. 'She was a great wee lassie', he said, 'She was a pet and she's dead. But I bear no ill will, I bear no grudge.'

Gordon Wilson became a potent symbol of love and reconciliation in a country torn apart by violence and hatred. In the years after Enniskillen, in his role as a member of the Irish senate, he continued to fight for peace until his death on 27 June 1995.

Activity

Reflection

Pupils should complete the following sentences.

A time when I needed courage was...

A time when I responded to something with violence or anger was...

A time when I responded to something with forgiveness and kindness was...

Prayer

The following prayer is based on the words of Philip Brooks.

Lord, we pray not for easy lives,
but to be stronger people,
we ask not for tasks equal to our powers,
but for powers equal to our tasks.

25 • Calling

Introduction

In the 1924 Olympic Games, an Englishman, Eric Liddell, qualified to run in the 100m final. Eric was very religious and it was part of his beliefs that it was wrong to compete in the race as it was being held on a Sunday. Despite a great deal of pressure, he felt he should withdraw from the final because of his beliefs. He switched to the 400m event. Although he had never competed in a 400m race in his life he went on to win the gold medal.

For Christians, a sense of calling or vocation is a strong awareness of being drawn by God to live your life based on Gospel values. Christians believe that each person is called to follow Christ in whatever way possible. In other words, in ordinary lives, to try to base actions and decisions on Christian values.

Scripture

The reading is from *Mark 2:13–17*. Jesus calls Levi, a tax collector. In the argument with the Pharisees Jesus stresses that all people, *especially* outcasts and sinners, are called by God.

> Jesus went back again to the shores of Lake Galilee. A crowd came to him, and he started teaching them. As he walked along, he saw a tax collector, Levi, son of Alphaeus, sitting in his office. Jesus said to him, 'Follow me.' Levi got up and followed him. Later on Jesus was having a meal in Levi's house. A large number of tax collectors and other outcasts were following Jesus, and many of them joined him and his disciples at the table. Some

teachers of the Law, who were Pharisees, saw that Jesus was eating with these outcasts and tax collectors, so they asked his disciples, 'Why does he eat with such people?' Jesus heard them and answered, 'People who are well do not need a doctor, but only those who are sick. I have not come to call on respectable people, but outcasts.'

Story

In his book, *Is that it?*, Bob Geldof tells of a journalist who describes Geldof as being called by God at a particular time for a special task – to help the poor of Africa.

'All of my life I felt like I had been waiting. For what I was unsure. Things felt good or bad but never complete. There was always something else – something unspecific. Not today. Had all the waiting been for this? Was this it?

"I think this must be the greatest day of my life," was all I could find to say. One journalist, writing in *Life* magazine, captured the unlikeliness of the whole affair with a vivid image. God had come down from heaven to find someone to undertake the task of alerting the world to the holocaust which was sweeping the continent of Africa. But this god, like the deities of old, bore the strength of fallibility and knocked at the wrong door. It was answered by Bob Geldof. "Who the hell is he?" thought God. "Oh never mind he'll do."

It seemed an unlikely business to me too. Nothing in my life, I would have thought, could have led me to this. I was a distinctly unsavoury and decidedly unsuitable person for such a vocation.'

Activity

Ask the pupils to reflect on and discuss the following questions.

Have you ever taken a stand on something because of your beliefs?

Have you ever felt 'called' to do a particular task?
Do you feel drawn by God to lead a particular way of life?

Prayer

The following Christian prayer is known as the 'Grail Prayer'.

Lord Jesus,
I give you my hands to do your work.
I give you my feet to go your way.
I give you my eyes to see as you do.
I give you my tongue to speak your words.
I give you my mind that you may think in me.
I give you my spirit that you may pray in me.
Above all, I give you my heart that you may love in me your Father and all mankind.
I give you my whole self that you may grow in me, so that it is you, Lord Jesus, who live and work and pray in me.

26 • Help

Introduction

'Give a man a fish and he has food for a day.
Teach him how to fish and he has food for a lifetime.'

(KUAN TZU)

Helping can be a dangerous thing.

It can be satisfying to have people come to us for help, to have people need or depend on us or to know that they are keen to listen to our advice. Helping someone may only serve to make them dependent on us. Helping someone may prevent them helping themselves. If we wish to help, and we should wish to help, then we must be sure that we are truly helping and really giving what people need.

Scripture

The reading is from *Matthew*. Jesus speaks of those who give freely to the hungry, the thirsty, strangers, the sick and the imprisoned. They will have 'His Father's blessing'.

When the Son of Man comes in his glory and all the angels with him, he will sit on his glorious throne, with all the nations gathered before him. He will separate people into two groups, as a shepherd separates the sheep from the goats; he will place the sheep on his right hand and the goats on his left.

Then the king will say to those on his right, 'You have my Father's blessing; come, take possession of the kingdom that has been ready for you since the world was made. For when I was hungry, you gave me food; when thirsty, you gave me drink; when I was a stranger, you took me into your home; when naked, you clothed me; when I was ill, you came to my help; when in prison, you visited me.'

Then the righteous will reply, 'Lord, when was it that we saw you hungry and fed you, or thirsty and gave you drink, a stranger and took you home, or naked and clothed you? When did we see you ill or in prison, and come to visit you?'

And the king will answer, 'Truly I tell you: anything you did for one of my brothers here, however insignificant, you did for me.' Then he will say to those on his left, 'A curse is on you; go from my sight to the eternal fire that is ready for the devil and his angels. For when I was hungry, you gave me nothing to eat; when thirsty, nothing to drink; when I was a stranger, you did not welcome me; when I was naked, you did not clothe me; when I was ill and in prison, you did not come to my help.'

And they in their turn will reply, 'Lord, when was it that we saw you hungry or thirsty or a stranger or naked or ill or in prison, and did nothing for you?'

And he will answer, 'Truly I tell you: anything you failed to do for one of my brothers, however insignificant, you failed to do for me.'

Story

Helping can be a dangerous thing!

A priest was walking down a street when he saw a little boy jumping up and down trying to ring a doorbell. The poor kid was too small and the bell too high.

So the priest went up and rang the bell for the little fellow. Then, turning to the kid with a smile, he asked, 'What do we do now?'

The little fellow said, 'Run like hell'.

Activity

In newspapers and magazines people write in for help with problems. Ask pupils to write a letter to God or someone they trust requesting help or advice with a problem they may have. Guidance may need to be given as to what sort of problem would be appropriate!

If the pupils are willing to have someone else read their letter then a friend could write a reply.

Prayer

The Prayer is from *Psalm 18*. The psalmist is thanking and praising God for the help and protection he has been given.

The Lord is my protector;
He is my strong fortress,
My God is my protection,
and with Him I am safe.
He protects me like a shield;
He defends me and keeps me safe.
I call to the Lord,
and He saves me from my enemies.
Praise the Lord!

27 • Failure

Introduction

We all make mistakes. Perhaps it is sports commentators who are most well known for theirs:

David Coleman: 'And they come through absolutely together with Wells in first place.'
Alan Weeks: 'This is the seventeen year old who has really plummeted to the top.'
Ron Pickering: 'He is going up and down like a metronome.'
Richie Benaud: 'The slow motion replay doesn't show how fast the ball was travelling.'

Whether mistakes are trivial, as in the examples above, or more serious it is easy to confuse them with failure. Failure comes not when we make mistakes or suffer setbacks but only when we give up wanting to improve or to move on. We only really fail when we refuse to learn from the mistakes we make or the setbacks we encounter.

Scripture

The reading is from *Mark 15:66–72*. When Peter denied knowing Jesus he must have been stricken with guilt and self-hatred at his lack of courage and conviction. We know that Peter learnt and moved on from this, probably the lowest point of his life, to become a man of great faith and strength.

Peter was still down in the courtyard when one of the High Priest's servant-girls came by. When she saw Peter warming himself, she looked straight at him and said, 'You, too, were with Jesus of Nazareth.' But he denied it. 'I don't know...I don't understand what you are talking about,' he answered, and went out into the passage. Just then a cock crowed. The servant girl saw him there and began to repeat to the bystanders, 'He is one of them!' But Peter denied it again. A little while later the bystanders accused Peter again, 'You can't deny that you are one of them, because you, too, are from Galilee.' Then Peter said, 'I swear that I am telling the truth! May God punish me if I am not! I do not know the man you are talking about!' Just then a cock crowed a second time, and Peter remembered how Jesus had said to him, 'Before the cock crows twice, you will say three times that you do not know me.' And he broke down and cried.

Story

Harry was very poor at his schoolwork; he could not read and could barely write. However, he was fit and strong. When he left school he eagerly applied for a job as a gravedigger. The local priest and parish council interviewed Harry for the job. Despite the fact that he was well liked and a hard-working young man he was not accepted – if he was unable to read, how could he distinguish the headstones? Harry was mortified; he did not know what to do. He had no skills, he didn't know how he could make a living.

As an act of kindness in his spare time Harry began to deliver groceries and milk to elderly neighbours. This grew and grew until it soon developed into a healthy living for Harry as a delivery boy and milkman. As the years went by Harry's business progressed and expanded to become the largest milk delivery service in the country.

When Harry came to retire he had established himself as one of the richest men in the land. On the day of his retirement Harry gave a rare interview to the press. They questioned him about his life and achievements. One reporter, having heard his life story, said to Harry, 'You've no qualifications, no proper education and you've gone on to such great success, have you ever thought of what you would have been if you'd have just learnt to read and write?' 'I've thought about that often,' Harry said, 'and I know exactly what I would have been – a gravedigger in a small parish church.'

Activity

Ask pupils to reflect on and discuss the following questions.

Have you ever made a mistake that you have learnt something from?
Have you ever picked yourself up from failure?

Prayer

We pray that in our successes we may be proud and yet humble and in our failures that we may struggle to learn and to grow.

28 • Peace

Introduction

On Remembrance Sunday we remember all the men and women who died during the two World Wars in their efforts to bring peace to our world. Today we each have opportunities to be bearers of peace. Not just a peace that is the absence of war but a peace in which there is justice, where there is freedom, and where there is equality. We can best remember and respect all those who died in the wars by being such bearers of peace.

Scripture

The reading is from *John 20:19–23*. Jesus has been put to death and the disciples are fearful of what the authorities might do to them. Jesus comes to bring peace to the disciples.

> The doors were closed in the room where the disciples were for fear of the Jews. Jesus came and stood among them. He said to them, 'Peace be with you,' and after saying this, he showed them his hands and his side. The disciples were filled with joy at seeing the Lord, and he said to them again, 'Peace be with you. As the Father sent me, so I am sending you.' After saying this he breathed on them and said, 'Receive the Holy Spirit. If you forgive anyone's sins, they are forgiven; if you retain anyone's sins they are retained'.

Story

On Christmas Eve of 1914 peace broke out. A group of German soldiers began to sing 'Stille Nacht' or 'Silent Night'. As the music drifted towards the British trenches, young soldiers joined in the singing and slowly the noise of gunfire was replaced with the sound of music. Germans and allies met and made peace for brief moments on that Christmas Day. Captain Sir John Hulse, of the 2nd Battalion Scots Guards, tells of these events in a letter to his mother.

> 'I climbed over the parapet and saw the strangest sight which can ever be seen by any soldier in any war. All along the line, groups of British and German soldiers were laughing and singing together. Just imagine it: English, Scots, Irish, Prussians, Wurtemburgers in a chorus. I wrote a report on the whole fantastic episode and ended by saying that if I had seen it on film I would have sworn it was a fake.'

Activity

The fields of France, once littered with the dead of World War I, reverted to fields of grass and poppies after the fighting had ended. The poppy has long since become a symbol of peace and a symbol of Remembrance Sunday.

The following instructions should be given to pupils.

Draw a poppy with two petals. Reflect on how you can be a symbol of peace in your own life. On one petal write how you could bring peace or justice to relationships in your family and on the other petal write about bringing peace and fairness to friendships. You may want to write about making up after an argument or about how you would want to treat your friends or family more fairly.

Prayer

In our prayers today we remember all those who have made sacrifices in order that we may enjoy peace and freedom. We thank all those who gave their lives in order to make the world a better place. May we learn to be people of peace and justice in every aspect of our lives.

29 • Advent

Introduction

Advent is the period of preparation leading up to the celebration of Christmas. In the busyness of the weeks leading up to Christmas Day much time is spent in choosing presents and organising celebrations. In the church Advent is a time of expectation – of looking forward to celebrating the birth of the child Jesus into the world. For Christians, Christmas is first of all the celebration that the eternal God has become a concrete reality in Jesus – God has come down to earth to meet us.

Scripture

The reading is from *Matthew 1:18–24*. The reading tells of the events leading up to the birth of Jesus. It recalls the words of the prophet who said that a child would be born and be known as Immanuel – 'God is with us'.

This was how the birth of Jesus Christ took place. His mother Mary was engaged to Joseph, but before they were married, she found out that she was going to have a baby by the Holy Spirit. Joseph was a man who always did what was right, but he did not want to disgrace Mary publicly; so he made plans to break the engagement privately. While he was thinking about this, an angel of the Lord appeared to him in a dream and said, 'Joseph, descendant of David, do not be afraid to take Mary to be your wife. For it is by the Holy Spirit that she has been conceived. She will have a son, and you will name him

Jesus – because he will save people from their sins.' Now all this happened in order to make what the Lord had said through the prophet come true, 'A virgin will become pregnant and have a son, and he will be called Immanuel, which means, "God is with us"'.

Story

The author of the following story uses a simple image to express his belief that Christians do not have to go up to meet God but that God, in Jesus Christ, has come down to earth to meet humankind. For Christians, Christmas is the celebration that God has come down to earth.

In the early days of television and plane travel, a young family was outside, on Christmas Day, making a snow-man. Suddenly a plane passed overhead. The mother shouted to all the children, 'That's the plane your uncle is on. Let's all wave. Maybe he'll see us.' The children jumped up and down and waved frantically, shouting at the top of their voices.

After the plane had passed over, the tiniest child turned to her father and asked, 'Daddy, how do people climb up to the sky to get into the plane?' The father explained that passengers didn't have to climb to the sky to get into the planes. The planes came down from the sky to the passengers.

Activity

Pupils should be encouraged to write the words for a Christmas carol. One possible theme could be 'God has come down to earth'.

Prayer

You were not born into influence and power, nor were you born into riches and luxury. You were born poor and powerless. You were born in this world in such a way that you came to meet each one of us.

We pray that this Advent, in our preparation to celebrate your birth, we remember the poor, the lonely and the powerless.

30 • Christmas

Introduction

The Christian festival Christmas is a time for giving and receiving gifts. The gifts that Jesus received from the Magi – Gold, Frankincense and Myrrh – are familiar to most of us. However the significance of the gifts is not as widely known. Frankincense would be used as an incense and would symbolise Jesus' role as a priest. Gold is precious and valuable; a gift fit for a king. Myrrh though is a spice or medicine. Myrrh is associated with pain and death. So in the story of the birth of Christ there is indication of his suffering and his death. Jesus was not to be a great warrior king, nor a majestic saviour, but a suffering servant who would die for others. At Christmas time, in the midst of all the celebrations, Christians remember the true meaning of the gift of the birth of Jesus Christ.

Scripture

The reading from *Matthew 2:1–11* tells of the birth of Jesus and the bringing of the gifts by the Magi.

> After Jesus was born in Bethlehem in Judea, during the time of King Herod, Magi from the east came to Jerusalem and asked, 'Where is the one who has been born king of the Jews? We saw his star in the east and have come to worship him.'
>
> When King Herod heard this he was disturbed, and all Jerusalem with him. When he had called together all the people's chief priests and teachers of the law, he asked them where the Christ was to be born.

'In Bethlehem in Judea,' they replied, 'for this is what the prophet has written: "But you Bethlehem, in the land of Judah, are by no means least among the rulers of Judah; for out of you will come a ruler who will be the shepherd of my people Israel."'

Then Herod called the Magi secretly and found out from them the exact time the star had appeared. He sent them to Bethlehem and said, 'Go and make a careful search for the child. As soon as you find him, report to me, so that I too may go and worship him.'

After they had heard the king, they went on their way, and the star they had seen in the east went ahead of them until it stopped over the place where the child was. When they saw the star, they were overjoyed. On coming to the house, they saw the child with his mother Mary, and they bowed down and worshipped him. Then they opened their treasures and presented him with gifts of gold and of incense and of myrrh.

Story

A great American storyteller wrote about two young people who were very much in love. Christmas Eve was coming and they wanted to give presents to one another. But they were very poor and had no money for presents. So each one, without telling the other, decided to sell their most precious possession. The girl's most precious possession was her long golden hair and she went to the hairdresser and had it cut off. She sold it then to buy a lovely watch-chain for her lover's watch. He, meanwhile, had gone to a jeweller and sold his watch to buy two beautiful combs for his beloved's hair. Then they gave their gifts. There were tears at first, and then laughter. There was no hair for the combs and no watch for the watch-chain. But there was something more precious and that was their self-sacrificing love for one another.

Activity

Ask pupils to consider a way in which they can make some form of sacrifice this Christmas – not just buying gifts but to genuinely give of themselves. Ideas may involve helping people within the community, collecting for hampers for the elderly and so on.

Prayer

We have nothing precious to offer, but we pray that we use the work of our hands to help the weak, the thoughts of our minds to bring light into the world, and the worship of our hearts to bring love to all.

31 • Beginnings

Introduction

When the fairytale princess stooped down to kiss the ugly frog we know that the frog was totally transformed. He became a handsome prince. The love of the princess had caused a dramatic change.

The start of a new year may not be as dramatic but it does provide opportunities for us to change; it gives us chances to start afresh, to make new resolutions, to grow.

The story gives us hope that, like the ugly frog, even dramatic changes are possible.

Scripture

The reading is from Paul's letter to the Ephesians. Paul is urging them to be transformed and made completely new in Jesus Christ.

'So get rid of your old self, which made you like as you used to – the old self that was being destroyed by its deceitful desires. Your hearts and minds must be made completely new, and you must put on the new self, which is created in God's likeness and reveals itself in the true life that is upright and holy.'

Story

About eighty years ago a man picked up the morning paper and, to his horror, read his own obituary! The newspaper had reported the death of the wrong man. Like most of us, he liked the idea of finding out what people would say about him after he died. He read past the heading which said, 'Dynamite King Dies', to the text itself. He read along until he was shocked to see that he had been described as a 'merchant of death'. He was the inventor of dynamite and he had grown rich through weapons that would kill and destroy. But he was moved by the description. Did he really want to be known and remembered as a 'merchant of death'? It was at that moment that a healing power greater than the destructive force of dynamite came over him. It was his hour of conversion. From that point on, he devoted his energy and money to works of peace and good works. Today, of course, he is best remembered, not as a 'merchant of death', but as the founder of the Nobel Peace Prize – Alfred Nobel.

Activity

The story of Alfred Nobel is a story of hope – 'I can change!'

Pupils should write a letter to themselves listing some of the ways in which they wish to change during this year. Included in the letter should be some of their ambitions and hopes for the year.

Prayer

For the ugly frog, love changed everything. At the beginning of this new year we pray, that love may transform our lives.

32 • Justice

Introduction

Jesus Christ was a man who was not afraid to speak out against any form of injustice. Throughout the gospels we hear of instances where Jesus challenged the beliefs and attitudes of others. Through His words and actions, Jesus taught about creating a Kingdom of God in which there would be equality and justice for all.

Many Christians have tried to follow the example of Christ and, in a peaceful and non-violent way, have made a stand against injustice. Martin Luther King, who was born on 15 January 1929, was one such Christian. Born into a culture where black people were discriminated against, segregated and victimised, he spoke out, proclaiming freedom and justice for all. It was his dream that black and white would 'one day live together as brothers' and that each person in the world would be 'judged on the content of his character rather than the colour of his skin'.

Scripture

The reading is from *Psalm 10*, 'A Prayer for Justice'. The Psalmist is praying to God, confident that He will side with the helpless and the oppressed.

> (Lord) you do see;
> you take notice of trouble and suffering,
> and are always ready to help.
> The helpless man commits himself to you;
> you have always helped the needy.

Break the power of wicked and evil men;
punish them for the wrong they have done,
until they do it no more.

The Lord is king for ever and ever.
Those who worship other gods
will vanish from his land.

You will listen, O Lord, to the prayers of the lowly;
you will give them courage.
You will hear the cries of the
oppressed and the orphans;
you will judge in their favour,
so that mortal men may cause terror no more.

Story

'I have a dream – that one day men will rise up and come to see that they are made to live together as brothers. I still have a dream this morning that one day every Negro in this country, every coloured person in the world, will be judged on the basis of the content of his character rather than the colour of his skin, and every man will respect the dignity and worth of the human personality.

I have a dream that one day...all God's children, black, white, Jews and Gentiles, Protestants and Catholics will be able to join hands and sing in the words of the black people's old song. Free at last, free at last, thank God Almighty, we are free at last!'

(MARTIN LUTHER KING)

Activity

Martin Luther King had a dream. In the style of Dr. King's speech pupils should write in their own words about their dream to create a fairer, juster and more peaceful world.

Prayer

We pray for strength and courage in our lives to make a stand against any form of injustice and inequality.

33 • Christian unity

Introduction

There are three main Christian groups, namely, Catholic, Orthodox and Protestant Christians. Within these there are over 20,000 different denominations. Many wars and much violence have been caused by the conflicts between these groups. However, in recent years there is great hope as developments in Christian unity gain momentum. The movement does not aim for all Christians to be the same but calls for people to recognise that each has perceptions of the one truth.

Scripture

The reading is from Paul's first letter to the Corinthians. Paul has realised that already there are divisions and arguments between groups of Christians. He calls each person to be united in the body of Christ.

'In the following directives I have no praise for you, for your meetings do more harm than good. In the first place, I hear that when you come together as a church, there are divisions among you, and to some extent I believe it. No doubt there have to be differences among you to show which of you have God's approval. When you come together, it is not the Lord's supper you eat, for as you eat, each of you goes ahead without waiting for anybody else. One remains hungry, another gets drunk. Don't you have homes to eat and drink in? Or do you despise the church of God and humiliate those who have nothing?

What shall I say to you? Shall I praise you for this? Certainly not! For I received from the Lord what I also passed on to you: The Lord Jesus, on the night he was betrayed, took bread, and when he had given thanks, he broke it and said, "This is my body, which is for you; do this in remembrance of me." In the same way, after supper he took the cup, saying, "This cup is the new covenant in my blood; do this, whenever you drink it, in remembrance of me." For whenever you eat this bread and drink this cup, you proclaim the Lord's death until he comes. Therefore, whoever eats the bread or drinks the cup of the Lord in an unworthy manner will be guilty of sinning against the body and blood of the Lord.'

Story

Many years ago in India six blind men came across an elephant. The first fell against the elephant's side and said to the others, 'I know what this is, it's a wall.' The second grasped hold of the elephant's tusk. 'No, my friend,' he said, 'it is round and sharp, it is a spear.' The third man did not trust the opinion of the first two and reached out for himself. He took hold of the elephant's trunk and jumped back in fright. 'It's a snake!' he exclaimed. The fourth man stretched out his hand and happened to touch the elephant's knee. 'It appears to me that this is a tree,' he claimed. The fifth blind man then brushed against the elephant's ear. 'This,' he said quietly, 'is a huge fan.' Finally the sixth man, still unconvinced, grabbed hold of the elephant's tail. 'You fools,' he shouted. 'Don't you know that it is a rope!'

Activity

Ask pupils to collect newspaper articles about the peace process in Northern Ireland where Catholics and Protestants are learning to live together in peace for the first time in twenty-five years.

They should write a prayer calling for the continued peace and unity of the people of Ireland.

Prayer

We ask that all people throughout the world learn to respect and accept their differences and learn to love and cherish those things that unite them.

34 • True love

Introduction

When we think of love, especially on Valentine's Day, we can think of romance, of chocolates and of flowers. However Christian love has little to do with sentimental giving. This sort of love has often been called 'tough love'. In other words, when Jesus Christ spoke about love, he talked of putting others first, of turning the other cheek, and ultimately of giving your own life for the sake of others. This sort of love isn't sentimental and gentle but is tough and uncompromising.

Scripture

The reading is from Paul's first letter to the Corinthians. It is probably the most famous section of *Paul* and represents the high point of his teaching. Here he says that above all else in the world the greatest of all things is love.

> 'I may be able to speak the languages of men and even of angels, but if I have no love, my speech is no more than a noisy gong or a clanging bell. I may have the gift of inspired preaching; I may have all knowledge and understand all secrets; I may have all the faith needed to move mountains – but if I have no love I have nothing. I may give away everything I have, and even give up my body to be burnt – but if I have no love, this does me no good.
>
> Love is patient and kind; it is not jealous or conceited or proud; love is not ill-mannered or selfish or irritable; love does not keep a record of wrongs; love is not happy

with evil, but is happy with the truth. Love never gives up; and its faith, hope and patience never fail.

When I was a child my speech, feelings, and thinking were all those of a child; now that I am a man, I have no more use for childish ways. What we see now is like a dim image in a mirror; then we shall see face to face. What I know now is only partial; then it will be complete – as complete as God's knowledge of me.

Meanwhile these three remain: faith, hope, and love; and the greatest of these is love.'

Story

The *Love is* cartoon strip appeared in the *Daily Mail* for many years. In one school staff and pupils were asked for their own ideas about what 'Love is'.

Love is...
believing in other people
feeling sick!
giving people your time when you haven't got any to give!
the total and unconditional acceptance of another as precious
really wanting what is best for others
being the first to hold a new-born baby
looking into the eyes of others and seeing the face of Jesus.

Activity

Pupils should draw their own *Love is* cartoon.

Prayer

The following extract is from *The Prophet* by Kahlil Gibran.

'When love beckons to you, follow him, Though his ways are hard and steep. And when his wings enfold you yield to him, Though the sword hidden among his pinions may wound you.

> And when he speaks to you believe in him, Though his voice may shatter your dreams as the north wind lays waste the garden.
>
> For even as love crowns you so shall he crucify you. Even as he is for your growth so he is for your pruning.'

This Valentine's Day, when we think of cards and gifts let us also remember the examples of love, of *true love*, that we have been given.

35 • Memories

Introduction

Life is so full and so busy that we take little or no time to reflect on where we have been in life and where we are going. We may do this with the practical elements of our lives but rarely with a wider focus. Does faith play any real part in our decisions and choices or is this irrelevant or neglected or merely tagged on as a sense of duty?

The purpose of the following exercise is simply to take time. To pause for a moment and give the pupils an opportunity to examine their lives so far – where has God been? And their hopes and fears for the future – where is God leading them?

If some staff feel uncomfortable with the explicitly religious style of this exercise, it is possible to use just the initial elements of the meditation.

Meditation exercise

PREPARATION

It is not possible to launch into a meditation experience with the pupils completely unprepared. The following notes may help with preparing the pupils so that what may be one of their first experiences of this quiet style of worship is enriching and leaves them wanting to know when they can do this again.

Timing and space are both essential elements. However, in reality, time is usually limited to set pastoral or registration periods and the space to a normal classroom. Run through the whole meditation exercise yourself at least once. A slow, steady pace is important with plenty of space allowed between each phrase to create the pictures or thoughts in their minds. Time it carefully, then use the most central part of the time available, thereby avoiding disruption by latecomers and ensuring that there is opportunity to discuss the experience after the meditation.

If the only available space is within the classroom use this space to its full advantage. Clear the desks to the sides. If the room is carpeted everyone can sit on the floor, if not on chairs. Sit in a circle with enough space between each person so that no one is touching anyone else. Place a candle, cross, icon or some other suitable artefact in the centre of the circle. Tell those teachers next door what is going to happen and put a notice on the door asking not to be disturbed during this time. Thus all outside disturbances can be reduced to a minimum and the best use made of the space available.

STILLNESS EXERCISE

The following 'stillness exercise' needs to be practised several times in its own right before leading into a meditation. This is just one way of many ways to reach the stillness and openness needed to reflect in this way.

Teach the pupils to sit well, ideally on the floor or on chairs with a straight back, yet relaxed not arched, with their hands still in their laps. All pens, pencils, bags, papers etc. should be left in another part of the room.

Once everyone is sitting in this way, ask the pupils to focus on a candle, or other object, or to close their eyes. Tell them to concentrate on their breathing and to breathe smoothly, silently and deeply. Guide the rhythm of their breathing, perhaps by counting.

Once this is established ask the pupils to listen to the noises outside the room, cars, children talking/shouting, footsteps, and leave these sounds behind. Do the same with the noises within the room, and then bring the pupils back to the rhythm of their own breathing.

After a while tell them to open their eyes and relax. *Always* encourage an open discussion following this or a longer meditation.

In My Life: a meditation

You will need:

cassette player, reflective music, *In My Life* by John Lennon candle, icon, cross or other religious artefact.

Prepare the room and the pupils in the usual way, tell them that following the stillness exercise this time you will guide their thoughts a little further. The Beatles song *In My Life* is appropriate for the end of this meditation. If you use this or another piece of music tell the pupils that the song is the last thing they will listen to and that they should remain quiet and still during this time too.

Begin with the stillness exercise and then slowly direct pupils' thoughts with the following statements.

Imagine you are walking down a beautiful tropical beach.

You can feel the warmth of the sun on your face...and your feet sink gently into the pure golden sand.

To your left are palm trees...you can see them moving ever so slightly in the gentle breeze.

To your right, the sea...a calm sea...listen to the sound of the waves gently lapping the beach.

You are relaxed and happy...and you lie down on the sand.

Let the sand run through your fingers.

Lying near you on the sand is a book, reach out and pick it up. It is a photograph album. Open it up.

[You will guide the group through the album. For each photograph ask them to look closely at each expression. What emotions are present at that time?]

The first photo is of you as a new-born baby, surrounded by your family. Everyone is smiling.

The second is a picture of you taking your first steps. Can you remember anyone telling you about times when you were only one or two? Something you said or did?

Turn the page in your album. You are now quite a bit older, it is your first day at school. Look closely at your expression. How did you feel on that first day?

The next photo is you as you are now. How has your expression changed? Are you happy or angry, enjoying life or under pressure from your family or friends?

You see yourself, to your surprise, getting married. You're smiling and everyone seems to be having a good time. How do you feel deep down?

You realise that you can now look into the future and eagerly you turn to the next page.

Here is a photo of you surrounded by your family. Is everything going well? Are the children smiling?

Turn the page again, you are now older. Your hair is grey and your face lined. Your own family have grown up and moved away. Look closely at your expression. Are you lonely, proud, full of hope or weary?

The final photo is of your funeral, your family are gathered around. Look closely at their expressions, the tears and sadness.

You are just watching the scene.

Your body is there but you are not.

You are suddenly aware that someone is coming towards you – it may be someone you love, a stranger or God. They ask you what you did in your life that was important. You pause and then give your answer.

What does the person or God say in reply?

You hear the sounds of the waves lapping on the shore again, and the warmth of the sun on your face. You are at peace.

Listen carefully to the words of this song. It's about someone looking back over their life and at their memories. (Play *In My Life* or another suitable song.)

After the music has finished allow the pupils to relax quietly and review the activity through an open discussion.

Extension idea

Put up a display entitled 'In My life'. Each pupil should bring in a photograph that holds a specific memory for them. Short written pieces outlining these memories could accompany the photographs on display.

36 • Uniqueness

Introduction

Each person is unique with a special and individual combination of talents, gifts and abilities. In all of creation there will never be two people exactly the same. But, if we are so special why is it that we get frustrated with ourselves? Why do we compare our looks, our intelligence, our abilities with those of others? We may be special but most of us certainly don't feel it!

This exercise is intended to help pupils to understand that they may not be the most intelligent, may not be the most beautiful, may not be the most talented but they are, and always will be, special and unique.

Pebble exercise

This seems an unlikely exercise and may appear trivial or silly or inappropriate to older pupils. However, because it addresses a fundamental aspect of our understanding of ourselves, it works! Sixth-formers and adults respond equally as well as younger pupils.

- You will need enough small pebbles for each person in the tutor group. Ask each person to choose a pebble.
- The pebble is the responsibility of the pupil for the whole week. They must take it everywhere they go: the pebble should be given a name; introduced to the family; be treated as a friend! The success of the exercise is dependent on the enthusiasm that is encouraged at this stage so it is important to regularly ask pupils about how they are caring for their pebble, the names they have chosen, and so on.
- At the end of the week pupils are asked to hand in their pebble. The pebbles are then mixed up, and, one by one, the

pupils are asked to come forward and, this time, to choose a pebble to keep. Invariably each person will recognise and choose the pebble that has been their own.

QUESTIONS FOR DISCUSSION

At the start of the week, what made you choose your particular pebble? Was your pebble the largest, or the smallest, the most rounded or the most perfect?

At the end of the week why did you choose your own pebble, not one that was a better shape, size or colour?

Will you keep your pebble? Why?

SUMMING UP

The exercise may be summed up using some or all of the points below.

The pebble that you chose to keep was one chosen from (thirty) pebbles, chosen from a beach of many thousands of pebbles, from a world of countless billions. And yet you chose yours because it was special, because it was unique. You chose it because you knew every aspect of its shape, every dent, every sharp edge, every colour. Many of you will keep hold of the pebble – it will become precious to you – it will be your own.

In a week we can learn to treasure a small piece of stone, not the most beautiful, not the most rounded, or the most colourful but just an ordinary piece of dull stone. Something that is worthless we can learn to see as precious. How much more should we consider ourselves to be precious and unique. We tend to look at others and compare. We look at others and see people more talented, more intelligent, more beautiful and more 'rounded'. We compare and then feel inadequate.

We should learn to look at ourselves in the same way as we have looked at the pebbles – we should learn to accept the dents, the sharp edges, the ugly aspects. We should learn to see ourselves as special, different, unique and *loveable!*

Extension idea

Suitable music could be used to reinforce the theme.

I Am the One and Only   Chesney Hawkes
Just the Way You Are   Billy Joel

37 • Forgiveness

Introduction

Apart from ourselves there are very few people whom we will totally accept just as they are, with their faults, failings, frustrating opinions and selfishness. There is a temptation to make demands, insist on changes, lay down certain conditions before we can accept or forgive someone. Then there are those who have deliberately hurt us, those who have been close to us but betrayed us in some way. Surely it is impossible to truly forgive these people?

In the two stories that follow, *The Yellow Ribbon* and *The Prodigal Son*, total forgiveness of another person unfolds.

Through these stories pupils will be encouraged to look at their own lives and focus on one person whom they find it difficult to forgive. In the story of the Prodigal Son pupils will have an opportunity to reflect on the unconditional love and forgiveness that God has for his people.

The Yellow Ribbon

You will need:

paper, pencils and a piece of yellow ribbon for each pupil (do not give these out yet), a cassette player and some quiet, reflective music.

Try to create a reflective atmosphere within the room, a stillness exercise (see page 112) and reflective music may help the pupils to listen more openly to the story. Also have a candle, cross or other artefact as a focus.

The story can be read by the teacher or prepared earlier and read in three parts: the narrator, the girl, and Vingo. It is essential that the story is read well.

The *New York Post* carried the story of a group of young people travelling by bus, on a holiday trip to Fort Lauderdale in Florida. Not long after leaving they noticed a dark-skinned middle-aged man, poorly dressed and looking quite worried, as he sat slouched in his seat, head down. When the bus pulled in at a roadside cafe, everyone got out except Vingo, as the young people had named him. The young people were curious about him – where had he come from, where was he going? Finally one of them sat next to him and said, 'We're going to Florida. Would you like some of my Coke?' After a while he told his story. He had been in a New York prison for four years. 'While I was there I wrote to my wife and told her that I'd be away for a long time, and if she couldn't take this, she should just forget about me. I told her not to write or nothing. And she didn't. Not for three and a half years.' Then he added, 'She's a wonderful woman, really good, really something.' 'And now you're going home, not knowing what to expect?' the girl asked. 'Yeah,' Vingo replied. 'You see last week when my parole came through I wrote to her again. I told her I would be coming by bus. As you come into Jacksonville, where we live, there's a big oak tree. I told her that if she'd take me back, she could tie a yellow ribbon on the tree, and I'd get off the bus and come home. If she didn't want me, forget it; no ribbon, and I'd keep on going.'

The girl told the others and soon they were all involved, looking at pictures of Vingo's wife and children, and all getting more anxious and nervous as the bus approached Jacksonville. There was a hushed mood in the bus. Vingo's face tightened. Then all of a sudden all of the young people were up out of their seats, screaming and shouting, crying and dancing. All except Vingo. He just sat there stunned looking at the oak tree. It was covered in yellow ribbons, twenty or thirty of them! The oak tree had been turned into one big welcome banner. As the young people shouted, Vingo rose from his seat, made his way to the front of the bus, smiled back at his young friends and got off.

In the same reflective atmosphere give out pencils and paper and guide the pupils' thoughts using the following (or similar) statements. Allow sufficient time between each.

Picture someone you have hurt, through something you have deliberately said or done, to anger or upset them. Put their name at the top of the paper.
Focus on the thing that you have said or done to this person. Write this down.
Picture someone that you need to forgive, someone who has deliberately hurt or upset you. What did they do to hurt you? Now write briefly about this.
Imagine meeting with them and telling them that you forgive them totally, unconditionally, you are willing to accept them just as they are. What do they say in reply?
Now write down the conversation between yourself and this person just after you have told them you forgive them. When you have finished this, roll up your piece of paper and tie your piece of ribbon around it. Quietly come forward and place your paper near the candle/artefact.

SUMMING UP
The exercise may be summed up using some or all of the points below.

You now have two people in your mind who can be totally forgiven, Vingo and the person you have written about. Vingo's wife lived out this forgiveness. Life, I'm sure, was not all sweetness and light in the days, months and hopefully years ahead. But at that vital moment Vingo's wife had enough love and forgiveness to offer an unconditional reconciliation, a new beginning. Without her forgiveness there would be no hope, no future.

Could you approach the person in your life? Maybe you need to talk together? Perhaps in the new way you treat them you can allow an unconditional reconciliation – a new beginning.

Reflection
Jesus told the story of the Prodigal Son to show the unconditional love that God has for each person. It is one of the most famous stories Jesus ever told. When you listen to the story put yourself in

the father's place. Would you be able to forgive the son after all the selfishness, betrayal, and thoughtlessness? Also put yourself in the place of the son. How would it feel to be totally forgiven, totally loved by your father?

Read *Luke 15:11–24*.

Jesus went on to say, 'There was once a man who had two sons. The younger one said to him, "Father, give me my share of the property now." So the man divided his property between his two sons. After a few days the younger son sold his part of the property and left home with the money. He went to a country far away where he wasted his money in reckless living. He spent everything he had. Then a severe famine spread over that country, and he was left without a thing. So he went to work for one of the citizens of that country, who sent him out to his farm to take care of the pigs. He wished he could fill himself with the bean pods the pigs ate, but no one gave him anything to eat. At last he came to his senses and said, 'All my father's hired workers have more than they can eat, and here am I about to starve! I will get up and go to my father and say, Father I have sinned against God and against you. I am no longer fit to be called your son; treat me as one of your hired workers.' So he got up and started back to his father.

He was still a long way from his home when his father saw him; his heart was filled with pity, and he ran, threw his arms around his son, and kissed him. 'Father,' the son said, 'I have sinned against God and against you. I am no longer fit to be called your son.' But the father called his servants. 'Hurry!' he said. 'Bring the best robe and put it on him. Put a ring on his finger and shoes on his feet. Then go and get the prize calf and kill it, and let us celebrate with a feast! For this son of mine was dead, but now he is alive; he was lost, but now he has been found.'

Extension idea

Role play a conversation between the Prodigal Son and his father the day after the celebrations.

38 • Image

Introduction

Most of us have two images, one we show to the outside world and one that is very personal, shared with one or two people or no one at all. There are very few people who have the courage to show this secret, true inner self to the world as this is us at our most vulnerable. Sometimes this inner self can become so obscured, so well defended that we begin to almost forget it ourselves. We can prefer to present a harder, perhaps more acceptable image to ourselves and the world. Here, pupils will be given the opportunity to focus on, or rediscover their inner image. Also to recognise that God knows this 'inside person', better, perhaps, than we know it ourselves. This mystery is expressed clearly by the author of *Psalm 139*.

'Your knowledge of me is too deep
It is beyond my understanding.'

On the outside: On the inside

You will need:
a large collection of newspapers, magazines and youth magazines, scissors and glue.

Each pupil will also need a shoe box or a large piece of paper (A3) folded in half.

Tell the pupils that the box or folded paper is to represent two images – on the outside the one they think the outside world sees and on the inside the image that is really them. Using pictures and perhaps headlines from the magazines and newspapers, they can cut out and stick appropriate images of themselves onto the relevant side of the paper/box. It would be helpful to spend some time discussing the idea of symbolism, so that each picture represents something. For example, a war scene may represent internal anger or family arguments, a mother and child may equal gentleness, and so on. This use of symbolism will increase the depth of meaning in the activity.

REVIEW

In small friendship groups ask the pupils to look first at the outside of each of their boxes and to explain the symbolism to their group. The group can comment on whether this is a fair image or if certain aspects of their character have not been portrayed. Then in the same groups repeat this activity, focusing on the inside of the boxes. Pupils could be encouraged to provide further insight into these inner images for others in the group.

SUMMING UP

The exercise may be summed up using some or all of the points below.

We have all studied two personal images, a superficial outer one and a deeper more personal inner one. If we have close friends maybe they already know us well, but perhaps through sharing and through your honesty you have deepened your friendships. There may be some things that are so special about your inner self that you have chosen not to share them; some may be good, some bad. However it is important to identify with our inner self as it, in turn, gives us inner strength and an ability to cope with the outside world.

Reflection

For centuries humankind has struggled with the idea of image, it is not something new to the end of the twentieth century. The author of *Psalm 139* expresses this dilemma clearly. There is a conflict between the outer image that the world sees and the inner image that he tries to ignore. He stands in awe of God, who truly knows and understands his inner self.

Read *Psalm 139:1–18, 23 and 24.*

LORD, you have examined me
   and you know me.
You know everything I do;
   from far away you understand all my
      thoughts.
You see me, whether I am working or
      resting;
   you know all my actions.
Even before I speak,
   you already know what I will say.
You are all round me on every side;
   you protect me with your power.
Your knowledge of me is too deep;
   it is beyond my understanding.

Where could I go to escape from you?
   Where could I get away from your
      presence?
If I went up to heaven, you would be
      there;
   if I lay down in the world of the dead,
      you would be there.
If I flew away beyond the east
   or lived in the farthest place in the
      west,
you would be there to lead me,
   you would be there to help me.
I could ask the darkness to hide me
   or the light round me to turn into
      night,
but even darkness is not dark for you,
   and the night is as bright as the day.
   Darkness and light are the same to
      you

You created every part of me;
   you put me together in my mother's
      womb.

I praise you because you are to be
     feared;
   all you do is strange and wonderful.
   I know it with all my heart.
When my bones were being formed,
   carefully put together in my mother's
     womb,
when I was growing there in secret,
   you knew that I was there –
   you saw me before I was born.
The days allotted to me
   had all been recorded in your book,
   before any of them ever began.
O God, how difficult I find your
     thoughts;
   how many of them there are!
If I counted them, they would be more
     than the grains of sand.
   When I awake, I am still with you.

Examine me, O God, and know my
     mind;
   test me, and discover my thoughts.
Find out if there is any evil in me
   and guide me in the everlasting way.

Extension idea

Keep the boxes, each one clearly labelled. Give them back to the pupils later on in the year, or if possible a year later. How have their images changed? Can they remember the symbolism they used? Have they more confidence to express their inner image?

39 • Speaking out

Introduction

It is very 'English' *not* to say what we feel. To do this can almost be regarded as weak. As a result many people grieve when someone dies, not only for the loss of someone they loved but for the missed opportunities to show by word or deed how deep that love was. Sometimes that grief is even deeper if it is partly the result of an unresolved argument or disagreement.

In his autobiography Brian Clough speaks clearly about this when writing about Peter Taylor's death. He states, 'Whoever said, "Never go to sleep on an argument" was right.' This sentiment is echoed in the song *The Living Years,* which tells of the unresolved differences between a father and his son.

Our teenage years of rebellion can often be the roots of such discord, here pupils will have the opportunity to reflect on the value of speaking out in a positive manner instead of in the usual more negative way.

Activity

You will need:

cassette player and *The Living Years* by Mike and the Mechanics (or alternative piece of music).

Create a reflective quiet atmosphere – music, a candle, cross or another 'centring' object may be helpful. You may wish to use a stillness exercise to create a listening atmosphere (see page 112).

As an introduction read out the following passage from Brian Clough's autobiography.

'If only Peter had come to my front door – I'd never have turned him away. That would have done the trick, buried the hatchet, melted the ice. I wish he had just called round for whatever reason. Any excuse would have been fine by me.

Such a notion is pointless, now, and a touch selfish on my part. Since Peter died I have come to realise that I should have been big enough to heal the breach. I should have driven to see him, or telephoned him. At the very least I should have answered or returned one of his calls on the occasions when he tried to get through to me at home. But you don't know people are going to go suddenly...

Given the benefit of hindsight we can all look back and say: "I should have done this, and I could have done that." It takes an event like the death of a friend to make you think in those terms. Whoever said "Never go to sleep on an argument" was right.'

In this special theme the pupils' experience of worship is deepened through the use of music. The song *The Living Years* fits well with the theme 'Speaking out'. The song could, however, be omitted from the activity or a suitable replacement found.

If appropriate, explain that a song will be played. Ask the pupils to listen carefully to the words, tell them briefly what the song is about.

Listen to *The Living Years*. (The lyrics of this song are reproduced on the opposite page.)

The pupils should think about their own families and friends (perhaps someone who has died). Is there anyone they need to 'speak out' to? Anyone they need to tell that they really care for them and why? Anyone with whom they need to sort out an argument?

Ask them to write a short letter to that person expressing these feelings. Some quiet music during this time may be helpful.

Every generation
Blames the one before
And all of their frustrations
Come beating on your door
I know that I'm a prisoner
To all my Father held so dear
I know that I'm a hostage
To all his hopes and fears
I just wish I could have told
him in the living years.
Crumpled bits of paper
Filled with imperfect thoughts
Stilted conversations
I'm afraid that's all we've got
You say you just don't see it
He says it's perfect sense
You just can't get agreement
In this present tense
We all talk a different language
Talking in defence
Say it loud, day it clear
You can listen as well as you hear
It's too late when we die
To admit we don't see eye to eye
So we open up a quarrel
Between the present and the past

We only sacrifice the future
It's the bitterness that lasts
So don't yield to the fortunes you
sometimes see as fate
It may have a new perspective
On a different day
And if you don't give up,
and don't give in
You may just be OK.
Say it loud, say it clear
You can listen as well as you hear
It's too late when we die
To admit we don't see eye to eye
I wasn't there that morning
When my father passed away
I didn't get to tell him
All the things I had to say
I think I caught his spirit
Later that same year
I'm sure I heard his echo
In my baby's new born tears
I just wish I could have told
him in the living years.
Say it loud, say it clear
You can listen as well as you hear
It's too late when we die.

SUMMING UP

The exercise may be summed up using some or all of the points below.

In the passage about Peter Taylor's death and the song *The Living Years* it has been someone's death that has caused the person to think about their true feelings, to regret the unresolved arguments and the times they have taken someone for granted.

Two close friends bitterly divided.

A father and a son who never seemed to agree on anything.

Both of these should tell us that we need to speak out and to express our feelings whenever we can.

Reflection

You will remember the tragedy at Hillsborough where 95 Liverpool football fans were killed. The short passage that follows was printed in the *Liverpool Echo* just after the disaster. It clearly states that we must live for today, tell people what they really mean to us and thank God for those we love. Pupils could be asked to spend a few moments in quiet prayer and thanksgiving after listening to the passage.

'The saddest fact of life is that it takes a taste of death to make you really appreciate the people you love.

On Saturday I was frightened and I thanked God for my family, something we don't do often enough.

Never let a good intention go by, never let a kind thought be forgotten.

All time is precious, all time has a value. We may fight because we care, but we do care. All fights must end with peace and apologies. This is what we forget. Life is too fragile and death is too definite...

If you love someone turn to them now not later and tell them. They need to know and there may not be a better time, there may not be any time.

To my family, I love you, and thank God for the safe return of my brother.'

(BRIAN FLYNN)